A NEW CAREER
AFTER FORTY

Starting Out...

A NEW CAREER AFTER FORTY

John C Bird

Northcote House

First Published in 1993 by Northcote House Publishers Ltd, Plymbridge House, Estover Road, Plymouth PL6 7PZ, United Kingdom. Tel: Plymouth (0752) 735255. Fax: (0752) 695699. Telex: 45635.

British Cataloguing-in-Publication Data.
A catalogue record for this book is available from the British Library.

ISBN 0-7463-0668-7
Typeset by PDQ Typesetting, Stoke-on-Trent
Printed and bound by BPCC Wheatons Ltd, Exeter

For Joan, an inspiration, and also a middle-aged career changer, and for David, Vivian and Julie.

Contents

Introduction

1   Routes to Change   **13**
Finding a job
Becoming your own boss
Returning to education

2   Managers and Advisers   **27**
Management and administration
Insurance
Financial adviser
Civil Service
Local government

3   Moving the Merchandise   **35**
Retailing
Sales and marketing
Transport and distribution

4   Changing Places   **49**
The opportunities
Architecture
Surveying
Estate agency
Building trades
Engineering

5   Classes and Culture   **53**
Teaching
Media and communications

Politics
Careers with languages
TEFL
Libraries
Museums
Archaeology

6 Healers and Carers   **65**
Health professions
Social, community and charitable work
Religious ministry

7 The Protectors   **91**
The legal profession
Security and protection services
Military service

8 The Living World   **97**
Rural pursuits
Careers with animals

9 Working for Leisure   **111**
The leisure industry
Arts administration
Travel and tourism
Boat services
Sports coaching
The hospitality business

10 Personal Services   **121**
Beauty and grooming
Driving services
Employment agency/Careers adviser
Introduction agency
Escort agency
Butler

Childminding
Funeral work
Genealogy
Graphology
Helping hand services

11 Creating and Performing 129
The visual arts
Conservation
Design
Crafts
Creative writing
The performing arts

12 Abroad Perspective 145
Working overseas
Emigration

Last Word 153

Useful Addresses 155

Further Reading 179

Index 189

Introduction

There is no security in this life,
there is only opportunity.

Douglas MacArthur

This is not a careers manual in the conventional sense, but a practical guide and a blueprint for action for the over-40s, which draws extensively on the actual experiences and advice of men and women who have themselves embarked on new careers in middle age.

It will be essential reading for anyone who has ever mused wistfully about 'quitting the rat race' or 'doing what I have always wanted to do before it's too late'. Even those who feel content and secure in their present employment owe it to themselves, in these uncertain times, to check out just what 'new start' opportunities might be available should their circumstances or ambitions change.

The restlessness and desire for change experienced by so many after 40 may be symptoms of the so-called 'mid-life crisis' during which members of both sexes try to come to terms with loss of youth, deteriorating looks and figure and diminishing libido, fear of the approach of old age, and, for women, that biological rite of passage, the menopause. It is time for assessing what has gone before, for setting new goals and finding a fresh sense of purpose, often in the shape of a new job or career. A variety of situations can provide the spur to action — redundancy or early retirement, the desire to escape from a rut or dead-end job, a broken marriage, the death of a partner, the so-called 'empty nest' syndrome, a sudden cash windfall, or simply the urge to fulfil a cherished ambition before it's too late.

As part of the research for this book I consulted a wide range of institutions and organisations in both the public and private sectors, and contacted several hundred individuals, many of them as a result of responses to my letters published in a variety of newspapers and trade and professional journals. Contributors include middle-agers from all walks of life who have taken up new occupations as artists, lawyers, nurses, writers, students, teachers, farmers, hoteliers, priests, shop owners, singers and driving instructors, to name but a few.

The sheer volume of contributions has inevitably necessitated considerable editing and selection. My aim has been to concentrate primarily on information and advice likely to be of most help to would-be middle-aged career changers. Accordingly most space has been devoted to those careers and occupations which are evidently of greatest interest to the over-40s, and to which they have the best chance of gaining entry, for example many of the health professions, farming and horticulture, and retailing. In addition, particular emphasis has been given to education because it is an essential preliminary to many careers. The creative arts, notably painting and writing, feature prominently because so many older people find fulfilment, if not always great financial rewards, from these pursuits.

'Middle age' has been variously defined, but for the purposes of this book, it has been taken to refer in particular to the years between 40 and 60. I have not, however, felt constrained from including helpful contributions from individuals marginally outside these rather arbitrary age parameters.

Sources of further information on each career are listed under Useful addresses starting on page 155, and suggestions for helpful further reading begin on page 179.

I would like to express my sincere gratitude to all the contributors whose generous assistance and advice have made this book possible.

John C. Bird
June, 1993

1

Routes to Change

FINDING A JOB

Finding the right job, any job, is often a difficult and frustrating process, which can be eased by adopting a sensible, carefully planned strategy.

First, check out the sections of this book which are appropriate to your career aspirations, including the *Returning to Education* section of this chapter if your target occupation involves a course of study; make use of the contacts in the *Useful addresses* section; note any relevant titles in the *Further reading* list and look them up at your local public library.

Use the various sources of advice available to you in a systematic way. This includes Jobcentres, the adult advisers based at many careers offices, and local colleges (some of which have mature student liaison staff). Your local Citizen's Advice Bureau can also be a helpful source of information and further contacts. In many areas 'Job Clubs' exist to help the longer-term unemployed find work. In the case of vocational careers, check out Employment Training (ET) — about to be re-named Training for Work — which is geared to suit the individual and offers the opportunity to gain a recognised vocational qualification or credits towards one; local Jobcentres have details. Also, get an information pack from the Training and Enterprise Council (TEC) in your area. The kind of qualifications you may need to consider are those approved or examined by such bodies as the Council for National Vocational Qualifications (NVQs), the Business and Technicians Education Council (BTEC), the Scottish Vocational Education Council (SCOTVEC) and the City and Guilds of London Institute. If you need financial help for vocational training ask about a career development loan (CDL) paid under an arrangement between the Employment Department and three leading banks (freephone 0800 585505 for further information).

Monitor the recruitment pages of the national, local and specialist press (you should find copies in your local public library) and sign on at your nearest Jobcentre and one or two private employment agencies. The Jobcentre will advise on various work finding initiatives funded by the Department of Employment.

Carefully prepared and well targeted speculative letters (to *named* individuals) can very occasionally produce positive results, but don't waste too much postage on this. Similarly, advertising your availability in the newspapers or trade press is not generally a very cost effective policy. Not all vacancies are advertised and who you know can sometimes be as important as what you know. Don't be bashful about making tactful use of the goodwill of any friends or acquaintances working in an occupation which interests you.

Ensure that any 'target' employer is left in no doubt about how your qualities and experience could benefit his or her organisation. Prepare, or have prepared, a typed and immaculately presented curriculum vitae (CV). Prepare meticulously for interviews — dress carefully, speak clearly, stay calm, and believe in yourself.

If you want to take your career in a new direction but are unsure which is the right one, you could consult one of the specialist firms which, for a fee, will assess your aptitudes, interests and personality, and counsel you on the most appropriate career choices. The London-based firm, *Career Analysts*, for example, offer among their various services a career review for people between 35 and 54 who want to 'stand back and think through very carefully what they want to do for the remainder of their working lives.'

CHECK LIST:

- Formulate a carefully targeted job finding strategy.

- Use all possible avenues of help, from statutory bodies and professional/trade associations to acquaintances in your 'target' occupation.

- Sell yourself as effectively as possible with a polished CV and careful preparation for interviews.

BECOMING YOUR OWN BOSS

One thing you will not be short of if you decide to go into business on your own account is advice. Literature covering every aspect of self-employment and small business operation, from tax and social security matters to funding and training is poured out by various government departments and agencies, business and trade organisations, banks and other commercial lenders. You will be able to pick up many of these publications at your local post office and library, as well as from the relevant organisations.

Make full use of the agencies which exist to help new businesses get off the ground. An invaluable source of advice is your local Training and Enterprise Council (the Scottish equivalent is a Local Enterprise Company). Check with them on the kind of training and financial help they provide for new businesses. If you have a viable plan which fulfils the criteria of your local TEC/LEC they could give you vital backing. If you live in a country area, the Rural Development Commission may be able to offer advice, training and perhaps financial help, providing your business is not agriculture or horticulture.

It is a fact that many businesses go bust every year, but thousands more succeed. Make sure that yours is in the latter category by getting the best financial and legal advice you can find, doing your homework on the competition, and carefully assessing the market potential for your product or service. Those planning to start a business in partnership with someone else should take particular care to get good legal advice in setting up the arrangements.

You are likely to find that banks and other lenders, though still keen for your custom, will be a good deal more cautious than in the recent past about handing out business loans. It is therefore more important than ever to prepare a sound, well thought out business plan, which should cover such matters as your experience relevant to the proposed enterprise, your financial resources, the size and potential of the market, the competitive advantages of your product, the stock and equipment needed to launch the venture, pricing and marketing proposals, and a revenue forecast. Be positive but realistic.

Your market research could include sending out questionnaires, calling in person or telephoning potential customers (prepare your questions carefully in advance), and consulting relevant businesses, local authorities and chambers of commerce.

Remember, all business involves risk. Sensible preparation is a vital step towards minimising that risk.

CHECK LIST

- Study the market and the competition, and satisfy yourself there is room for your product or service.

- Develop a business plan and get sound financial advice as early as possible.

- Make full use of the agencies which exist to help businesses get started.

RETURNING TO EDUCATION

Mature students

An academic or professional qualification is an essential prerequisite for many careers, and in some cases this may involve a full-time course at a university or other institution of higher education. Many mature students opt for full-time study, even though part-time alternatives may be available, in order to enjoy a higher education in its widest sense, making it their 'day job' and immersing themselves in their studies and a completely new way of life.

This section focuses particularly on the experiences of full-time students, although much of the information and advice applies equally to those taking part-time courses.

If you decide to go for a place in higher education, be prepared for keen competition for entry to most full-time degree courses. However, even if you have no formal academic credentials and haven't done any serious studying for years, your chances of acceptance may be better than you think. Most institutions are prepared to waive or modify their standard entry requirements in the case of mature students.

Your admission prospects will depend on a variety of factors, including the length of the course, its cost to the taxpayer, the demand for places from younger applicants, your life and work experience, and your educational background. Not surprisingly, you have a much better chance of acceptance for, say, a three-year arts degree than a medical or dental course, which involves five or six years of training.

Traditionally the polytechnics (which in 1992 acquired university status), colleges of higher education and their equivalents in Scotland, have recruited many more older students than the established universities, but the latter have stepped up their efforts to attract 'matures' in recent years. It is not simply that demographic trends are reducing the number of 18-year-olds, or because of the desire of institutions to increase their incomes by boosting course numbers; the higher education community has other reasons for welcoming older students, which are reflected in these comments from tutors and admission officers:

They are a highly desirable category. They are 'streetwise', having studied in the 'university of life', and usually have a more balanced perspective of issues. *(City of London University)*

Because of their commitments and enthusiasm, tutors regard older students as good role models. We believe that their wider life experience enriches their younger colleagues. *(Anglia Higher Education College, Cambridge)*

Mature students are frequently the liveliest contributors to seminars and debates, and the most interesting to teach. *(University of North London)*

Often they assume a quasi-parental role. *(St Andrews University)*

This section is devoted mainly to men and women who have taken, or at the time of my research were taking, full-time courses in the arts and social sciences — probably the most popular and accessible choices for the over-40s. Because certain problems tend to be common among mature students regardless of their field of study, much of the advice and the issues discussed here are also relevant to later chapters, which are concerned with qualification in such fields as teaching, law, social work and the health professions.

Finding a course
Once you have decided, at least in general terms, what you would like to study, the next step is to do a little research to find an institution, either locally or further afield, which offers the kind of course you want, and what their entry qualifications are.

Several excellent handbooks and directories are available which offer comprehensive listings of the kind of information you need to help you make your choice. You should be able to find many of these publications in the reference section of your local public library. The Department of Education and other bodies also issue free leaflets containing up to date information on such vital matters as students' allowances and advice for mature students.

In many parts of the country there is a free Educational Guidance Service for Adults (EGSA), which provides help and information on education and training opportunities. Among the sources to which it has access is *ECCTIS 2000*, a comprehensive database listing courses and the qualifications needed for entry.

Adult students with family and property commitments generally prefer to study at an institution within reasonable travelling distance of their homes, providing it offers the course they wish to follow. Once you have identified the place which you think might be right for you, telephone or write to the undergraduate admissions office and obtain a prospectus. Study this carefully and critically, together with any separate literature which might be available on the specific course or courses that interest you.

If you are going to spend three or more years in a place, the physical location is an important consideration. This may vary from cramped, shabby buildings in a city centre to a modern purpose-built campus in a semi-rural area, a converted stately home or the almost museum-like colleges to be found in Oxford and Cambridge. Any institution, naturally, will wish to promote itself in the best possible light, so if you are not familiar with the location, go and look it over and get the feel of the place. Find out if they are having an open day: this would enable you to see more and talk more freely to staff.

If you have a partner or dependents you may wish to check if any family accommodation is available. What sort of sports and leisure facilities are there? Is there a mature students society? What is public transport like if you need it? What social amenities are available in the area?

Qualifying for entry

Once you have found what you feel is a suitable combination of course and location, write to the admissions office of the institution concerned telling them what you would like to study and setting out your personal and academic background, work experience and any other qualifications likely to strengthen your case for entry.

Because the backgrounds of mature candidates vary so widely, it is usual for each application to be assessed on its merits and you will probably be invited to attend an advisory interview with the admissions tutor for the course in which you are interested. The session is likely to be friendly and sympathetic and will involve consideration of your strengths and weaknesses to help the tutor to reach some conclusion about your ability to cope with the course. A member of Kent University's registry staff told me, 'In the case of middle-aged applicants we are less concerned with previous qualifications than with establishing that the candidate has the commitment and intellectual capacity to complete a degree course successfully.'

If you have not done any fairly concentrated studying for some years, you will probably be advised to take an *Access* course (more about this option later) or some other kind of preparatory study.

Some institutions may ask you to submit work samples in the form of essays or book reviews, build up a portfolio of experiential learning, or take aptitude tests.

Whatever the outcome of your initial contacts with an institution, in most cases you have to make a formal application for admission through a central clearing system. Most applications for places in higher education are handled by the University Central Council on Admissions (UCCA) and the Polytechnic Central Admissions System (PCAS), to be merged in August 1993 to form the Universities and Colleges Admissions System (UCAS).

Pre-entry courses
A variety of study options are open to mature students seeking to prepare themselves for degree courses. Some take GCSE and A levels or equivalent courses, such as ordinary national certificate (ONC), higher national certificate (HNC) or BTEC certificates; others obtain Open University credits, opt for 'Access' or 'Return to Study' courses run by local colleges and universities, or perhaps attend a diploma course at an adult residential college.

GCSE and A level courses can be taken at local colleges, either part-time or full-time, or through a home learning course with an institution such as the National Extension College (NEC). The NEC offers a wide variety of courses up to degree level, and almost 30 per cent of its students are over 45. Some courses are based on the *flexistudy* system which combines correspondence work with face-to-face tuition at a local college. A list showing courses available at various correspondence colleges can be obtained from the Council for the Accreditation of Correspondence Colleges.

For some the battle to qualify for university entrance is anything but easy. A Hampshire contributor began an O level English course after being discharged from his third period of treatment as a chronic alcoholic. 'I was regarded as a hopeless case,' he said. 'I was illiterate, my physical condition was poor, and I was listed as brain damaged.' Despite these problems he got his GCSE pass, went on to take two A levels, and followed up with a university-run/ 'Return to Study' course. He was subsequently offered places at two universities, accepting one of them to begin an English degree at the age of 58.

Access courses are specifically designed for mature students with few or no formal qualifications who may not have undertaken concentrated study for some years. A typical course might run over three terms, but may be extended over two years with hours to suit the student. The training includes a core element covering basic academic skills, such as essay writing and study techniques, and a number of subject options which are chosen by the student in accordance with the kind of higher education course he or she is hoping to follow. Assessment is likely to be by a mixture of assignment marks and examinations at the end of the course.

'I would recommend an Access course as an excellent introduction to essay writing, note taking and also as a confidence builder,' said Lily, a family doctor's wife, who took this kind of course before beginning an MA honours degree in philosophy at Dundee University at the age of 43. 'I feel the course was a far better preparation for university than the courses taken at school.'

One of the attractions of attending an adult residential college is that it offers older students a chance to sample 'campus life' before going on to full-time degree courses. Adult residential colleges are located at Barnsley, Birmingham, Dalkeith, Harlech, Loughborough, Surbiton (women only), and Oxford, where there are two colleges. The courses are usually of one or two years duration and include subjects such as literature, history, social studies, economics, computing, politics and psychology. No formal entry qualifications are required and adult bursaries paid direct by the Department of Education are available to cover costs. Many students also obtain funding from other sources, such as their trade unions.

Robert had been unemployed for two years when he began a course at Coleg Harlech in Wales. After completing it he obtained a place at Durham University, where, at 44, he graduated with first class honours in psychology and anthropology, and then went on to research for a doctorate. Alan, a former car industry worker and union shop steward, embarked on a two-year history diploma course at Ruskin College, Oxford, after being made redundant at 59. He subsequently took a degree in history and politics at Oxford Polytechnic.

Paying your way
Some mature students have few financial worries during their courses, perhaps enjoying private means or being supported by their partners or families. For many, however, paying their way can be a continuing worry, though most survive to complete their courses.

The problems are likely to be exacerbated if the student has to move away from home to get a place on the course he or she wants. Even with state or charitable help, some contributors reported spending all or most of their savings and having to borrow money from friends and relatives. The absence of government benefits during vacations adds to the difficulties, especially for students with dependent children.

If you are entering full-time higher education for the first time you should qualify automatically for an award from your local education authority. This will include tuition and other fees and an element for maintenance for yourself and any dependents. To qualify for this so-called mandatory award the course has to be designated, ie approved by the Department of Education, and you must have lived in the UK for three years up to the September before you begin your studies. Should you not fill the Department's criteria for a mandatory award your Local Education Authority (LEA) may be able to offer you a discretionary award, which could have conditions attached such as requiring you to attend an institution in your local area. The cash value of LEA maintenance grants are frozen at the 1990-91 levels, although top-up loans at fairly attractive interest rates are available under a government sponsored scheme to all full-time home students on approved higher education courses (apart from postgraduates) up to the age of 50. A spouse's income is also taken into account in assessing a grant. Some institutions offer fee concessions to those who enrol after retirement age.

If you can't get local authority help you may be able to obtain assistance from one of a number of educational trusts and charities; the Carnegie Trust and the Wills Trust are two such organisations. A number of directories, such as the Directory of Grantmaking Trusts and the Charities Digest, contain useful information on sources of charitable aid for students. Some universities and colleges have hardship funds which may be able to offer modest assistance.

Making ends meet during a three-year course can be particularly hard for single parents, as Christine, a nurse, discovered while studying for a BA degree in combined studies at the Humberside College of Higher Education. Aged 45, with three children, when she began, she found her financial problems were compounded by 'endless difficulties' with the local council over housing benefit. After running up an overdraft at the end of the second year she had to work three night shifts every weekend at a nursing home throughout the final year of the course. She graduated with upper second class honours and looked on her degree as a reward for 'years of poverty, cultural isolation and general deprivation which seem to be the lot of the modern British female single parent.'

Coping with the course

My survey of institutions around the country suggested that in most cases mature students cope with the academic demands of their courses as well as and sometimes better than their younger counterparts. However there appear to be certain common problems which many older students experience, such as these cited by course tutors:

> Older students often lack confidence when they start, but most emerge well qualified and with a new confidence in their achievements. *(Teesside University)*

> They experience anxiety over grades, getting back into essay writing, revision and examination techniques. *(University of East Anglia)*

> Many need coaching in study skills and learning how to learn. *(Hertfordshire University)*

> Not all, but many, do too much work, for example trying to do a research project on every essay. *(Reading University)*

> Those that drop out usually do so for non-academic reasons. *(West Sussex Institute of Higher Education)*

Problems most often cited by the students themselves were concerned with lack of confidence, difficulty in memorising material and organising studying and revision efficiently. Here are some reactions from students who tackled these problems successfully:

> I came with no academic qualifications and was very low in confidence, but I applied myself to the task, and came first in the class in psychology and got the faculty prize for course work and examinations in political science. I was totally shocked by this as I always had the feeling I was struggling. *(former dance teacher taking degree in psychology, philosophy and political science at Dundee University)*

> It is important to organise study hours and stick to them. Also, if possible, have a certain place to study where you don't do any other activity. *(housewife taking psychology degree at the University College, North Wales)*

> I treated my course like a job, and liked to put in a full day's work. If you find learning difficult at first, you will get better with practice. Work hard at it, but take plenty of short breaks to give your brain a rest. *(former technical sales manager who took BSc*

and PhD degrees in chemistry at Nottingham University)

Fitting in

Generally middle-aged students seem to get on well with their younger counterparts and members of staff, though they are often considerably older than both.

During his history course at the University of East Anglia, Alan, a former oil company executive, found relations with students of all ages very easy, but felt the presence of a significant number of other mature students was nevertheless a help. 'It is essential to forget old ideas about hierarchy in order to relate to other students and faculty,' he said. 'It is also important to understand the role of "argument" in discussion. Too much personal involvement with one's own opinions, the desire to be always right and have the last word will be a disaster. Learn to ask questions again.'

Lady Elspeth Howe, wife of the former deputy Prime Minister, Lord Howe, took a degree in social science and administration at the London School of Economics in her early fifties, and had no problem fitting in at an institution which has a tradition of welcoming both women and mature students. She found her fellow students kind and helpful and made some good friends who she still sees. 'A mix of bright young minds had some plusses in class situations, and tutors were helpful,' she said. In the second and third years of her course her husband's duties involved her in considerable travel and entertaining. 'By burning the candle at both ends and with help from fellow students, eg by taking my recording machine to the lectures I missed, I survived,' she said. 'It was a pressurised but very enjoyable experience.'

The social dimension

Because of the age gap between themselves and the majority of students and many staff, and the fact that so many of them live at home during their courses, middle-aged students often miss out on the social activities which can be an enjoyable part of college life, and some report experiencing a sense of alienation. There is no evidence, however, that those who choose to participate in student social life get anything less than a friendly reaction from most of their younger counterparts.

Robert, a graduate student at Durham University, believes that many older students neglect the social side of student life because they regard it as inappropriate for their age and experience. 'I feel that is a mistake', he said. 'In my second and third years my social experience of student life was as important as my academic experience. Student social life provides a fundamental context for academic achievement, and in my opinion is more important than interaction with lecturers.'

Living in university accommodation during her philosophy course at Sheffield University, Christine, a former home care worker, found that although she encountered no particular difficulties in relations with other students and tutors, she often felt alienated 'as I didn't fit in anywhere.' She believed it was important for mature students to belong to or form some kind of support group.

Family matters
Trying to balance academic and domestic demands is a common dilemma for the mature student with dependents. Lack of support and understanding by partners can sometimes create almost intolerable pressures on a student who may be struggling to keep the family finances afloat while at the same time trying to keep up with course work. Equally difficult tensions can develop when the student fails to show adequate consideration for the feelings and needs of his or her family.

Traditional role expectations often mean that women students are more likely than their male counterparts to face difficulties in juggling conflicting domestic and study commitments. More than a few women encounter the 'Educating Rita Syndrome' with partners continuing to expect the kind of attention and service to which they had become accustomed.

Margaret, a former radiographer who graduated from Sheffield University at 49 with an honours degree in economic and social history and sociology, stressed the need for sorting out priorities before starting a course. 'If the family is paramount, forget it,' she said. 'Particularly for a woman there must be a clear undertaking that a full-time course is just that — not something mum is amusing herself with while carrying on looking after the family. This doesn't mean they need to feel neglected; my lot knew exams and essays were important because I related my experience to what they were undergoing at school. We shared the joys of good marks and consoled each other with the not so good. The main thing is to be organised, but flexible and committed. It's worth it when the whole family rolls up to your graduation and rounds off the day with proud grins on the official photograph.'

Male mature students with young children can also face acute family pressures. During his mathematics degree course at Imperial College London, Nick, a further education college lecturer, had to take two separate years off to cope with the needs of his family. 'I began the course with two children,' he said, 'but we had twins after a year of the course. I had no grant or other public funding, I got £300 from a charitable trust and had to use up an inheritance, sell the house and buy a cheaper one. My wife had to work flat out and had a nervous breakdown. Whenever the children were ill I stayed at home. I was only able to attend 50 per cent of lectures at best, and was very seldom able to turn up for tutorials.' Despite these pressures, Nick graduated with honours.

How it changes you

Many middle-aged graduates find that their experience of higher education significantly changes their perspective on life and affects their relationships with members of their immediate family and friends.

'No-one warned me how much I would change,' said Susan, a former computer programmer with a large engineering company, who took a BA in theology at Birmingham University. 'I began to lose a lot of what I had in common with family and friends. I was very disappointed after such a 'high' to revert back to the mundane routine of life.'

Changes in his outlook and personality became a source of strain in the marriage of a workshop technician who followed up an Open University degree with an MSc from Sheffield University. 'My wife was still the girl I married,' he said, 'but I was no longer the man she married. My life came to include things she couldn't share. I also made friends with people to whom she couldn't easily relate. These things caused considerable friction and required great effort on both sides before they could be contained.'

You're never too old!

Many graduation ceremonies have been graced in recent years by men and women in their sixties and older.

Eugenia, a former administrator in a charitable Home for the Aged, was 66 when she collected an upper second class honours degree in history and English from the University of North London. She found that the age difference of more than 40 years between her and most of her fellow students proved totally irrelevant. One of her reasons for taking the course was to 'overcome the slur of ageism and the stereotyping of older people often imposed by our society and passively accepted by many of my generation.' She dismissed as meaningless the injunction to 'act your age'.

'Retirement offered us the chance to do exactly what we wanted with the rest of our lives, but it took us some time to realise that this was to study,' said John, a former customer relations manager with an electrical appliance firm. He and his wife Rita enrolled on a humanities degree course at the University of the West of England and found their studies 'stimulating, satisfying and a wonderful confidence booster' when they found that they could cope just as well as 18-20 year olds.

Others who have demonstrated that you're never too old to become a full-time degree student include Jean, a former geriatric worker who began a philosophy degree at Leeds University at the age of 66; Agnes, a retired post office official who was the oldest graduate when, at 63, she stepped up to receive her MA in English and social administration at Dundee University; John, a former porter who earned a BA in humanities from the University of Greenwich at 62; Paul, a retired businessman who took a BA in philosophy at 64 and followed up with an MA and, at 73, a PhD; and Elizabeth, a former financial executive who was 76 when she embarked on her humanities degree at the University of Greenwich.

CHECK LIST

- Choose your course carefully in terms of location, content and also assessment method.

- Remember that most mature students do as well as or better than their younger counterparts.

- If you have dependents, be prepared for difficulties in trying to balance family and academic demands.

2

Managers and Advisers

MANAGEMENT AND ADMINISTRATION

Portable skills

Management and administrative skills are portable and adaptable, and they have enabled many middle-agers to switch to fields often quite different from those in which they have previously worked.

For those seeking to expand or update their skills, and perhaps further increase their marketability by obtaining formal qualifications, a variety of courses is available from BTEC up to postgraduate degree level. Many of the professional organisations for men and women working in specialist areas of management also conduct certificate and diploma courses. A well recognised general qualification for managers in all types of businesses is membership of the British Institute of Management (BIM), which also provides a useful forum for information and contacts. If you have no formal qualifications, the BIM may admit you as a member on the basis of extensive experience in management.

Company secretary

Experience in such areas as administration and accountancy can provide a springboard towards that key position in any firm, the company secretary.

The qualification awarded by the Institute of Chartered Secretaries and Administrators (ICSA) is also recognised for administrators in local government. The standard entry requirements for the ICSA training programme may be relaxed for mature entrants with relevant experience. It is not uncommon for students to begin preparing for the Institute's examinations in their forties, and some start as late as their sixties. The examination scheme includes modules in such subjects as economics, accounting, law, information systems, personnel administration and management. You are expected to complete the programme within five years, although an extension may be allowed in special cases.

Work study
This is a promising field for late starters with solid industrial or commercial experience. A diploma or certificate course with the Institute of Management Studies can be taken by part-time or correspondence study over three years.

Computers
Computers are a vital tool of modern management. Many older people, brought up on more traditional methods of dealing with data, have been diffident about adapting to new technology. However, increasing numbers are training to use them either as a matter of necessity to retain their jobs, or to increase their marketability in seeking new career opportunities.

Beginners courses in computing geared to the needs of mature people are available at many further education colleges. Word processing is a popular option which many over-40s find helpful, not only for business purposes but also for use at home in letter writing and routine record keeping.

Clerical and secretarial work
Many over-40s made redundant or taking early retirement use office skills acquired in their former careers to find full-time or part-time clerical work. More enlightened employers are less concerned with the age of applicants than their ability to handle the necessary tasks efficiently, and this may require some keyboard familiarity. There are good prospects for returners and late starters as secretaries, personal assistants and in similar appointments because qualities such as maturity, calmness under pressure and reliability, often lacking in the younger generation, are valued by employers.

For those who want to sharpen up old skills or acquire new ones, a variety of courses is available at local further education colleges. The most marketable qualifications include those from the Royal Society of Arts (RSA) and London Chamber of Commerce and Industry (LCCI). Subjects offered include business, secretarial and office studies, information technology and languages.

Management consultancy
Many middle-agers make use of the expertise, training and contacts acquired in business and industry over many years to forge new careers as consultants and advisers. With a growing number of businesses 'buying in' expertise, the scope for consultancy work

continues to expand in such fields as management, engineering, computers and investment.

Among those I heard from was Tony, a robotics expert who set up a management consultancy after the automation firm he worked for went into receivership. In his new venture he specialised in 'the development of strategic objectives and/or technical solutions related to the manufacturing, health-care and food industries.' In collaboration with his wife, who has special expertise in health-care related activities, he has built up a clientele that includes both small firms and large government-supported organisations. Although there have been times when they have had too much business and periods when there has been too little, Tony said that they have made more money than they could have done as employees, and achieved a lifestyle which provides greater freedom of choice.

Redundancy was also the spur for Peter, an electrical engineer, to apply his talents to consultancy. Initially he specialised in the energy efficiency field, but later switched to environmental matters. He has also written several books and contributed articles to the technical press. Now past retirement age, he is still working enthusiastically and said he is learning all the time.

Accountancy

Becoming professionally qualified in one of the main branches of accountancy involves several years of study and supervised on-the-job training. The main difficulty for late starters is likely to be that of finding a firm prepared to take them on and provide the necessary training.

A survey of employers conducted on behalf of the Institute of Chartered Accountants (ICA) in England and Wales revealed that the majority of firms were prepared to consider mature applicants, but many of them looked for exceptional qualities before accepting anyone over the age of 30. Positive attributes of older entrants cited in the study were that they tended to be more easily accepted by clients, had more commitment, fitted into office life more quickly and easily, possessed an element of commercial awareness, and had readily apparent social skills. On the negative side there was evidence that mature students were more likely to 'drop out' and some appeared to have a struggle with their studies.

The training syllabuses of the major branches of the profession, such as chartered, certified, financial and cost accountancy, are similar in many respects though the emphases may differ. If you want to explore prospects further, contact the ICA's Student

Education Department.

A shorter training — BTEC or correspondence course — is involved in becoming an accountancy technician. The breadth of responsibilities in this occupation are somewhat less than those of a qualified accountant, but prospects are quite good for late entrants. Contact the Association of Accountancy Technicians for more details.

It is possible, of course, to offer accountancy and bookkeeping services without formal professional qualifications, but you are precluded from activities regulated by the government, such as auditing company accounts, insolvency work and giving investment advice.

Among the successful late starters I heard from were a former Metropolitan policeman who retired with 25 years service, trained as a financial accountant and became tax manager with a firm of chartered accountants; an ex-banker who qualified in accountancy after retirement and took over the books of some of his old customers, and a retail executive who turned to bookkeeping after being made redundant, qualified as a financial accountant, and became an adviser to several companies.

INSURANCE

Salesperson

Middle-aged recruits are sought after by the insurance industry, and especially by those companies selling life cover and products such as pensions and investment plans. They know that the over-

40s can bring such qualities as maturity, *gravitas* and a sense of responsibility which inspire confidence and receptiveness in potential clients. Also, the older recruit with a background of many years in commerce or industry is likely to have built up a network of contacts, many of whom might be converted into clients. A commercial or accounting background makes the mature candidate even more attractive to the insurance companies, whose job advertisements often specifically target the over-40s.

Broker

To set up your own insurance brokerage you need to have acquired some experience in the industry, perhaps with a major insurance company or an established broker. You are required to register with the Insurance Brokers Registration Council, which means having at least five years experience, or three years if you have passed the examinations to earn associate membership of the Chartered Insurance Institute. Those who want to handle life insurance must be members of LAUTRO (Life Assurance and Unit Trust Regulatory Organisation Limited) or FIMBRA (Financial Intermediaries, Managers and Brokers Association).

This is what some latecomers to brokerage had to say:

> After completing 28 years with the police I went to work for an insurance broker. I did a one year part-time course on the basics of insurance and attended various residential courses with selected insurance companies. Two years later I started my own consultancy with the intention of having a one-man office. Within three months I had to engage a full-time secretary, and then took on two representatives. I am now a Fellow of the Institute of Insurance Consultants, and we are also independent financial advisers. I would advise anyone thinking of entering this field to start planning two years beforehand. Visit a brokerage, talk to insurance company representatives, embark on a course of study, and then maybe try for an agency with one of the major insurance companies. *(retired police officer)*

> I set up in business at 44 and quickly decided to concentrate on marine business. It takes longer than you think to build up a business, perhaps double the time you would estimate beforehand. Plan carefully and realise luck (good or bad) will affect business. I was lucky to choose yacht insurance at the time I did. I now know of other lines I would take up if I

wanted to. I use manual records on card and paper, having found no convincing reason to buy a computer. *(former clerk in life assurance company branch office)*

I developed from a direct salesforce person into a wider brokerage situation to take on more life companies and expand into motor, house contents, etc. Do not be tempted by high potential incomes based on commissions only; it is an extremely stressful way to begin working in the business. *(former engineer in the aircraft industry)*

FINANCIAL ADVISER

This is a potential option for mid-life career changers with experience in business and commerce. To be able to work in this field you must be licensed by one of the regulatory bodies, FIMBRA or LAUTRO. You are required, not unreasonably perhaps, to be solvent, trustworthy and without a criminal record.

Obviously the success of a financial adviser will depend heavily on the quality of advice given, and the confidence and trust built up with clients. Much of the business is likely to come through personal recommendations, discrete advertising and attending conferences, seminars and other 'contact making' events. A good grounding for those planning to set up as independent advisers is to work for a spell with one of the large investment services companies, selling their range of products on a commission basis.

The advisers from whom I heard came from backgrounds as varied as banking, the motor industry, the Civil Service, the oil industry, building societies, and stockbroking. In addition to their advisory work, some also use their expertise to run investment clubs, teach at local colleges, write newsletters and do research for stockbrokers.

Iain, a former marine telecommunications specialist who began working on a freelance basis for a major investment services group after being made redundant, told me 'The problems include having to do too much "cold calling", closing sales and trying to make a liveable income. Some clients resist advice that does not offer short-term gain. But there is much pleasure in achieving solutions to clients' needs. Pre-research at least 400 potential customers and test the opinions of acquaintances as to whether they would deal with you once you start your new career. Do not approach close friends until some practical experience has been gained. Be prepared to face a slow build up of income and have enough put aside to support outgoings before you begin. Warm up prospective clients rather than seeking immediate business. Never forget that clients have friends and long memories: they can refer or they can deter others.'

CIVIL SERVICE

Despite sizeable staff cutbacks in many departments during recent years, the Civil Service continues to provide a variety of opportunities for mature entrants with appropriate technical, professional or administrative skills.

All recruits must fulfil nationality requirements — normally you must be British or Irish — and the maximum entry age depends on the class into which you are recruited. There are no age limits for those entering as administrative officers or administrative assistants, who handle mainly clerical work; executive officers must be under 50, but late entry to the top level administrative class is possible for high calibre people up to the age of 52. Such candidates with relevant professional experience in, for example, architecture, surveying, economics or science, may be recruited into specialist branches of the Civil Service, including Her Majesty's Inspectorate of Taxes. The selection process, involving interviews and tests, is rigorous.

LOCAL GOVERNMENT

There is no formal upper age limit for entry to local authority administrative and clerical posts, and previous experience of administration or working with the public is a plus which may earn exemption from standard academic entry requirements. Some local authorities are more flexible than others in balancing a job applicant's past experience with his or her academic record or lack of one.

Local authority structures vary according to the type of area covered, but in addition to clerical and administrative staff they employ a wide range of professionals such as architects, engineers, accountants, lawyers and librarians.

CHECK LIST

- Management and administrative skills can be adapted to many different fields, and are particularly valuable to those starting up their own business.

- Maturity and commercial awareness are qualities especially sought after in the insurance industry.

- The Civil Service and local government provide a variety of opportunities across a wide range of professions, but selection standards are high.

3

Moving the Merchandise

RETAILING

A popular option

If, as Napoleon is supposed to have remarked, England is a nation of shopkeepers, then a considerable proportion of them seem to be middle-aged career changers.

Retailing is a popular option because the capital outlay involved is within the means of many who want to run a small business of their own. Also it can have an agreeable social aspect, with the opportunity to get to know customers and become a valued member of the local community. With a few exceptions, such as chemists and opticians, no formal qualifications are required, though several contributors recommended trying to get some experience assisting in a shop before setting up on your own.

There are increasing opportunities for the over-40s to obtain retail experience in larger outlets, both on a full- or part-time basis. Some of the major retailing chains, such as Tesco and B&Q, operate positive policies to encourage older recruits. Tesco ran an experimental mature entrant programme in the late 1980s and was so impressed with the results that it launched a national campaign on the theme 'Life Begins at 55'. This attracted a substantial number of older staff, and Tesco has found that:

- most of them have an in-built regard for providing a high standard of service;
- their absenteeism rate is low; and
- their stability sets a good example to younger staff.

Similar benefits from employing the over-50s have been experienced by the DIY retailers B&Q, who reported:

- reduced staff turnover;
- improved timekeeping;
- greater confidence in dealing with difficult customers; and
- better standards of service.

Staff vacancies are often advertised in the stores themselves as well as in the local press.

The rest of this section is aimed primarily at those interested in the possibility of buying their own retail business.

Antiques

There is ample opportunity for the shrewd latecomer to enter the antiques trade, but you need to tread with caution until you have learned the ropes. In this business there is no substitute for experience, and even the experts occasionally burn their fingers. You can start in a small way, working from home buying and selling antiques at auctions and car boot sales. Then, as you build up experience and stock, you could try taking a stall at local markets and antique fairs.

From the outset you should soak up all the information you can find from books and periodicals, and tactfully pick the brains of other dealers in their shops and at auctions. As well as becoming well versed in the historic and technical background of antiques, you need also to be able to haggle effectively with other dealers and customers. Attend as many auctions as you can, carefully observe everything that goes on, and file the catalogues with the sale price marked against each item.

In due course, if you feel sufficiently confident to risk the hefty investment on stock, you could consider opening a shop, but this would require some careful research beforehand on the potential market and competition in the area.

Once you have become well established as a bona fide dealer you could seek membership of one of the trade's professional bodies, The British Antique Dealers Association or the London and Provincial Antique Dealers Association.

Bakery

The kind of domestic baking experience acquired over the years by many homemakers can provide a useful basis to build on, particularly for a smaller, more personalised business. If you buy an existing business try to persuade the vendor to let you spend at least a few weeks working alongside him or her to learn the tricks of baking on a larger scale and also the financial aspects of the operation.

You have to get up very early to start baking each day's stock, but you can build a faithful band of customers if you offer them a range and quality of products more to their liking than that found at supermarkets. Many bakers also boost their takings by running an in-house café. Most learn on the job, but a variety of courses are available to help develop your skills and acquire some formal qualifications. Check with your local further education college.

Bookshop

My research indicates that bookselling is a popular choice with the over-40s. Some opt for general bookshops, others specialise in areas such as military history or children's books, and one contributor operates a successful postal service for books on theology and church history.

Here is a distillation of the advice contained in the responses I received from contributors in many parts of the UK:

- Try to get some experience working in a bookshop before starting out on your own.

- Draw up a business plan.

- Position is all important; try to find premises where you will be noticed.

- Research your market, your catchment area and the competition. If in a university town, for example, make the appropriate contacts and stock relevant academic books. Develop links with the local schools and the public libraries so that you can serve them as a supplier.

- Explore the possibilities of exporting and mail order business.

- Specialise; it will help you withstand the competition from the big retailers.

- The credit terms imposed by publishers will probably mean that, unless you have a very rapid turnover, you will need an overdraft. Do not underestimate the possible level of this.

- Be ruthless with stock and return non-selling items as soon as possible, and eliminate non-selling categories. Do not overstock: this will probably mean taking a firm stance in dealing with persuasive publishers' representatives.

- Be prepared to order books for customers: this builds up goodwill and a growing clientele of regulars.

- Be willing to use a computer.

- Dismiss the notion, which continues to have currency, that running a bookshop is a gentle and pleasant activity to while away your mature years. Be prepared to work extremely hard and put in long hours on such matters as maintaining your accounts and keeping abreast of new titles.

Christmas is the best time for business. You are likely to meet some interesting people even if you don't make a fortune. While you can get your initial stocks from a wholesaler, you will need to register with the Booksellers Association to get supplies from publishers. The Association runs courses useful to newcomers to the business.

Butcher

This is not the kind of shop to open without having some background in the trade. If you don't have this, it might be possible to get some hands-on experience with an established butcher under the Employment Training (ET) scheme. Also check out the Institute of Meat's training programme.

As a small independent butcher, you need to know both your cuts and your customers' requirements thoroughly to have a decent chance of surviving against the strong competition from the supermarket chains. This will almost certainly mean offering something special, for example meat from organically fed animals, or game, and a first-class personal service, perhaps including home delivery.

The initial capital outlay is sizeable on such essential items as freezers, chopping blocks and implements, but providing vegetarianism doesn't become too popular, there will continue to be a good living to be made by the high class family butcher who is just that.

Clothing and fashion

This is the kind of business which needs not only flair — particularly with a boutique — but a substantial investment in stock. Without previous experience of selling clothes or in some other branch of retailing, the learning curve can be steep and initial outlay expensive. Some middle-aged newcomers from other backgrounds nevertheless choose this kind of shop, learn fast and do well. This is what two of them had to say:

> We run a ladies and men's boutique selling casual to smart wear for the mid-market. Cash flow is always a problem, but the business has given me independence and I have been able to earn more money than most women of my age coming back into full-time work. This is still one of the few fields where a woman is not at a disadvantage. (*former journalist*)

I deal mainly in dance and exercise wear, including shoes and a small range of leisure wear. I thoroughly enjoy the variety of buying the stock, serving in the shop and doing the paperwork, which is endless. I made a good profit at the end of the first year, but it's not a 'get rich quick' business. *(former department store buyer)*

Confectioner, tobacconist, newsagent (CTN)

If you are prepared to work long hours and like the idea of getting to know a large number of people in your locality, then a CTN shop might be just up your street.

Whether located in a small village or on a busy town high street, this kind of shop is likely to have a fairly brisk flow of customers and a rapid turnover of many relatively low-cost items. In addition to the familiar range of confectionery and tobacco products, newspapers and magazines, items stocked by CTNs may also include toiletries, groceries, small chemist items, and services offered may range from video hire and printing of personal stationery to photocopying and photographic developing. Most of these shops also provide home delivery of newspapers.

Although some contributors cited such problems as inefficient wholesalers, staff shortages, absenteeism among newspaper deliverers, and the necessity to rise at the crack of dawn and work late, this type of shop remains one of the most popular choices among middle-agers entering the retail trade. Here is how some of them see their move into CTNs:

Newsagencies appeared to be the most profitable opportunity in retailing, and were comparatively cheap to buy, but I worked four years in another newagency before buying my own. Profit comes mainly from news, but we have diversified into groceries, stationery, greeting cards and toys. I have been able to substantially increase turnover and profitability. The main problems have been with news wholesalers, who have tended to give a very poor service. *(former electronics firm executive)*

It has been very hard work, especially at the beginning. I get up at 4 am seven days a week and handle 600 publications and over 600 accounts. I read the trade magazines thoroughly for information and new ideas, and attend local meetings of the National Federation of Newsagents, which have saved me many a pound. *(ex-teacher)*

The takings initially were approximately 50 per cent of those advertised. By the end of the year we had increased takings by 50 per cent. We did this by improving and increasing stock, obtaining an improved overdraft facility, and providing a first-class service to our customers. We monitor our expenditure with a computerised bookkeeping programme and have helped give the business a more professional image through the purchase of a van advertising our name. We employ one full-time person (43 hours a week) and seven part-timers (varying hours). Between us my husband and I work 203 hours a week. *(former local government official)*

Do-it-yourself/hardware
Despite fierce competition from the major chains of DIY superstores, many smaller shops still flourish by providing a knowledgeable and more personal service in their communities.

The proprietors I heard from have shops in locations ranging from small villages to the London suburbs, and their stocks reflect the wide range of lines traditionally carried by such outlets, for example fancy goods, wet weather clothing, fuels, timber, tools, gardening equipment, electrical and plumbing accessories, pet foods, computers, security equipment. Some offer such agency services as picture framing, furniture renovation and dry cleaning.

Here is a summary of their advice:

- Study the competition carefully — there is an awful lot of it, but don't be frightened of the major retailers, the so-called shed-operators; they cannot be beaten, but they can be lived with, and the market has adjusted to their arrival.

- Make sure you arrange adequate finance, with cover for emergencies over and above the expected cost of the business and stock.

- Ensure you have plenty of suppliers, and try to search out some lines that can be exclusive to you in your area.

- Beware of stocking too many slow moving lines.

- Be prepared to work seven days a week in the early stages.

This kind of business is really a way of life suitable only for someone prepared to make a strong commitment.

Florist

Floristry is a growth industry in more ways than one, and offers a chance to provide not only a personalised service, but one with a touch of creativity and artistry. Apart from supplying suitable designs for weddings, funerals and other occasions, the florist visits flower markets and nurseries to select stock from all over the world, and arranges displays for hotels, offices, exhibitions and so on.

'People of more mature years have little difficulty in mastering the techniques of floristry,' says the British Retail Florists Association. 'With experience and with correct instruction they emerge frequently as skilled and proficient florists'.

Floristry courses are provided by many further education colleges, and most welcome mature students.

Jeweller

A considerable background of specialised knowledge needs to be built up in order to establish a successful jewellery business. Many acquire this through reading, attending specialist auctions, and buying and selling jewellery on a part-time basis. Helpful part-time and correspondence courses are available from the National Association of Goldsmiths and the Gemmological Association of Great Britain. As the experience of even the major chains of jewellery stores has demonstrated, however, during recessionary times this branch of the retail trade can suffer more than most.

It is possible to keep overheads much lower by taking space in one of the permanent or regular indoor markets around the country or by participating in craft and antique fairs, rather than opening a shop.

Gwen, a former interior designer and her husband, who run a jewellery outlet in a London antique emporium, have built up a thriving business by specialising in gifts. 'I took a course in jewellery making and silversmithing for one year to learn the basics of the trade,' she told me. 'I run the shop and do the buying and display, and my husband does all the administration. There is immense satisfaction in knowing we are choosing the right products for our customers. We have no shop window and so rely on customer satisfaction and recommendation.'

Off-licence

Not for the temperance enthusiast (or the tippler!), an off-licence is a challenging option for late starters who are not afraid of competition. Some combine this kind of business with a grocery or general store.

Tom, who opened an off-licence and general store after winding up his catering company, runs a single shop on an estate of some 500 houses, opening from 9am to 9pm on Mondays to Fridays with shorter hours at the weekend. 'There is very limited opportunity to take time off for holidays,' he said. 'You have to guard against the danger of overstocking due to the variety of customers' requests. The satisfactions include the opportunity for self-expression in the variety of goods stocked and the standard of service you provide.' He advised: 'Research the market thoroughly both for growth and competition. Particularly plan in detail for the second and third year and make monthly projections on cost and income for one year ahead. Monitor projects vigorously and adjust regularly. Be prepared to work hard and long hours. Family involvement is essential.'

Sub-post office

Much sought after, particularly in rural areas, sub-post offices are often integrated with a confectioner, tobacconist, and newsagent (CTN) or general store.

You have to convince the Post Office of your reliability and financial soundness before they will allow you to purchase a sub-post office. If the selection panel gives you the nod, the Post Office provides initial training and pays a salary in accordance with the number and type of transactions carried out.

There is no upper age limit, but unless there are no other suitable applicants, candidates over 60 are unlikely to be appointed. Previous experience in the Post Office or in retail, banking or clerical work would be advantageous, says the Post Office, but is not essential. For further information contact the district manager of Post Office Counters Ltd. in your region.

Here is a selection of comments from contributors who took over sub-post offices after 40:

Total commitment is essential, otherwise you will almost certainly fail. You must learn everything there is to know about your business. The main satisfactions are helping people with investment and other problems, introducing new products (providing they are successful), analysing the progress of the business and comparing this with previous years. I am also a dealer in first day covers and other philatelic items. (*former banker, Avon*)

The main problem is red tape. Small shops provide a living for the proprietor, but not if you're supporting a bank. There's no fortune, but it's a glorious way of life. Be prepared to give up holidays. (*ex-journalist, North Wales*)

The premises are in a shopping parade (16 units) on a large housing estate. The business is more financially rewarding than teaching and provides a continually changing social/work situation. There's no time for boredom. (*former teacher, Tyne and Wear*)

CHECK LIST:

- It is wise to get some experience in a shop before buying one of your own.
- Carefully assess local competition.
- Be prepared for long hours, especially in the early days.

SALES AND MARKETING

Sales agent

The best preparation for going into business as a sales agent is field experience on the sales force of one or more reputable companies. Most agents represent several clients and often work from home. The job can involve considerable travel and long hours, but income can be high once you become successfully established, and some agents do so well that they have to take on assistants.

Ann, a former sales representative on the staff of major pharmaceutical and cosmetics companies, who became an independent agent selling imported drugs, gifts, films and cameras to retail chemists, advised:

- Allow at least six months before expecting to earn a reasonable income.

- Only handle products that will give repeat business.

- Only work for companies that pay commission 'on invoice', not on payment from customers, otherwise you could wait months for your money.

- Try to handle five agencies to begin with. Take on more when these are established.

- The first 12 months are the hardest, and there is a lot of competition. If you survive, you'll never want to go back into employment.

A variety of sales training courses are available part-time and by correspondence. Check first with your local further education college.

Marketing consultant

Your age shouldn't be a problem if you want to become self-employed as a marketing consultant, but you will need a good track record to attract quality clients.

The kind of experience required for success is likely to include senior marketing posts with major companies or top marketing firms. Some international experience, a language or two, and some evidence of intellectual capacity, perhaps a degree or professional qualification, will also strengthen your hand.

Franchises

An increasingly popular option for those wanting to run their own business is a franchise in which an organisation allows you to produce and/or sell goods or services using its business name and provides the back-up of advice and management and marketing experience. The terms of the deal may include help with such matters as site selection, construction of premises, training, and in some cases allow exclusive coverage of a particular territory. In return the franchisee usually pays an initial licensing charge and continuing fees, often in the form of royalties on sales.

Franchise opportunities range from carpet cleaning and car tuning to running a shop, restaurant or hotel. Some franchises are run by individuals while others, which may involve major capital outlay, could have a number of joint investors. Well-established and reputable franchise operations, such as Wimpy, Kentucky Fried Chicken, Hertz, Dyno-Rod and Prontoprint, offer the considerable trading benefits of a nationally known name and the expertise built up over years of operation of similar outlets.

Not all franchisors are as scrupulous and efficient as the famous names just mentioned, however. If you are tempted by blandishments about exciting business opportunities with high profits and low risks, proceed with caution. Don't make any commitment without taking legal and financial advice, and if possible talk to a franchise consultant. Assure yourself on the following points:

- How long has the organisation been established in the UK?

- How does its product or service compare with the opposition in quality and price?

- What is the extent of the actual, not just the promised, back-up, for example with regard to advertising, publicity and training?

Ask the franchisor for the names of some existing franchisees, then contact them and ask them in as much detail as tactfully as possible about their experience with the organisation; in particular, how far has the franchisor lived up to his predictions on turnover and profits?

The good news if you decide to take on a franchise is that statistically you are much less likely to fail than if you set up a totally independent business. Research sponsored by a major bank indicated that only five per cent of franchisees fail compared to 25 per cent of go-it-alone businesses.

Export

Some late changers, whose previous careers have involved experience in fields such as overseas sales and representation of foreign companies in the UK, are able to use their know-how and contacts as a basis for starting their own export business.

If you want to explore the possibilities, helpful and up-to-date information can be obtained from the British Overseas Trade Board or one of the Department of Trade and Industry's offices located at various centres around the UK (see your local telephone directory).

A related option is freight forwarding, which involves acting on behalf of exporters and importers to arrange collection and delivery of goods.

Market research

Organisations of all kinds, from charities and political parties to local businesses and multi-national corporations, have a voracious appetite for information about their 'rating' with their customers and consumers. Such data can be an important aid to marketing and management policy.

Attitude surveys among potential consumers have become increasingly sophisticated in recent years, and there is a continuing demand for researchers to collect the data by such means as telephone, door-to-door or street interviews. For much of this work, maturity and experience can be distinct assets. The work is by its nature mostly part-time and advertisements for researchers often appear in the press.

Potential employers include the Office of Population, Censuses and Surveys (OPCS) and the market research agencies and contractors who carry out surveys on behalf of client organisations. If you are hired as a researcher on a part-time or casual basis, you will usually be given training, and courses may extend to two or three days.

CHECK LIST

- Competition in a sales environment can be tough; a good track record helps.

- *Always* take legal and financial advice when considering a franchise.

- Market researchers are always in demand, although much of the work is part-time. Maturity is frequently a distinct asset and training is often provided.

TRANSPORT AND DISTRIBUTION

Road transport

The upper age limits for drivers of heavy goods vehicles are a matter for individual companies. A heavy goods vehicle licence (HGV) is required, and you need to be fit and quite strong, particularly if working with the larger vehicles.

Your chances of acceptance for training as a bus or coach driver will vary according to the recruitment policy of the company or operator concerned, though generally no formal upper age limits are laid down. You have to pass a fairly demanding test to obtain a public service vehicle (PSV) licence enabling you to drive a vehicle with nine or more seats used for hire or reward. Lighter commercial vehicles can be driven on a full ordinary driving licence.

(See also the section on Driving Services in chapter 10.)

The railways
The popular childhood dream of becoming a train driver usually fades long before middle age, but if it hasn't there is still at least a theoretical possibility of realising it. Providing you are under 46, British Rail is prepared to consider you for training to work on its trains. For station and yard staff there is no specified upper age limit, but BR requires all candidates to pass a medical examination.

If you run into the buffers with BR, you could make tracks elsewhere. London Underground does not impose any formal maximum age restriction, though you would be unlikely to be taken on over the age of 62. Other possibilities are the Dockland Light Railway in London, Glasgow Underground, and the Newcastle Metro.

Going to sea
If a life on the ocean wave is on your list of desirable careers, don't be in too much of a hurry to pack your cabin trunk.

The Royal Navy has little room for the over-40s and your chances of being welcomed aboard by the shrinking Merchant Navy are small, unless you happen to be an itinerant entertainer, musician, sports coach or lecturer on a popular subject, in which case you might get some occasional work on cruises.

Recruitment policy is controlled by individual companies, so if you are determined to try your luck, you could perhaps contact one or two of the larger shipping lines. If you live in or near a seaport, you might put in a call to the Merchant Navy Establishment Office there.

Should all else fail, you could (if you can afford it) take a navigation course and buy a boat of your own; sign on as a deck or galley hand on someone else's vessel, or perhaps console yourself with a trip to sunnier climes on a banana boat (the Geest Line offers just the thing).

Post Office
The Post Office will consider candidates up to the age of 45 for its graduate recruitment scheme. Counter staff are recruited up to 55, and commercial and office experience are particularly welcome.

The formal upper age limit for postmen and women is 59, but entrants are normally below 45. Candidates have to pass an aptitude test and interview. Contact your local postmaster for further information.

Courier services

A number of independent courier services exist to provide rapid delivery of documents and parcels locally, nationally or to destinations overseas. Couriers may travel by bicycle, motor cycle, van or aeroplane.

Maturity and reliability could be an asset in finding this kind of outdoor employment, but you need to be fairly fit and mobile, especially for local delivery work. A number of air courier firms offer much reduced fares to world-wide destinations if you are prepared to carry packages for them.

Consult the *Yellow Pages* for courier firms in your area.

4

Changing Places

THE OPPORTUNITIES

Much of the work of the professions and trades considered here involves changing the face of the landscape and the man-made structures within it. They are concerned with such functions as measurement, design, development, construction, management, repair, maintenance, decoration and selling of property.

Most of these occupations offer opportunities for self-employment, working in consultancies or with organisations in either the private or public sector, including the Civil Service.

ARCHITECTURE

This is one of the tougher professions for the over-40s to break into, not least because of the lengthy training involved. To be able to practice as an architect in the United Kingdom you must get your name on the register maintained by the Architects' Registration Council of the UK (ARCUK). This means passing examinations set by the Royal Institute of British Architects (RIBA), which normally involves a five year course and two years on-the-job training with a ARCUK-recognised firm.

Whether you remain employed by an existing practice or in due course strike out on your own, making a name for yourself can be a long haul, unless perhaps one of your buildings comes to the notice of that outspoken architectural observer, the Prince of Wales.

Shorter training is required to become an architectural technician, and is perhaps a more viable option. The British Insitute of Architectural Technicians will provide details.

SURVEYING

Many older people are probably well equipped for the meticulous and thorough approach which is necessary in much of the surveyor's work. Your chances of late entry to the profession are likely to be improved by experience in a relevant field, such as construction. Course entry requirements may be relaxed for older applicants.

There are a number of branches within the profession, concerned with such areas as building and quantity surveying, agriculture, minerals and mining, valuing and auctioneering. Many surveyors also work in estate agencies.

To practice as a chartered surveyor you have to be accepted as a member of the Royal Institution of Chartered Surveyors (RICS), and qualification involves a course of degree level academic study, spending two or three years as a probationary trainee in a practice, and passing a professional examination. You can also qualify, rather more quickly, as a surveying technician through BTEC courses. For information contact the Society for Surveying Technicians.

ESTATE AGENCY

There are no formal barriers to prevent the over-40s from becoming estate agents, but those who have aspirations to open their own agencies would be well advised to get some hands-on experience first. Professional qualifications are needed to be able to undertake surveys and valuations.

The Residential Estate Agency Training and Education Association advised that older entrants could often succeed because of the maturity and perceived *gravitas* they brought to an estate agent's office. Formal academic qualifications are not essential, but employers look for 'intelligent, articulate applicants who combine a willingness to work hard with enthusiasm and integrity, and a real interest in matching buyers' needs with the characteristics of properties listed.' Experience in such areas as building management, sales and administration would be looked on favourably.

Some estate agents and surveyors specialise in auctioneering, concentrating on, for example, property and land, art and furniture, or plant and machinery.

Full-time and part-time courses to qualify for membership of such professional bodies as the RICS and the Incorporated Society of Valuers and Auctioneers (ISVA) are offered at local colleges, and also by correspondence through the College of Estate Management in Reading, Berkshire. Many earn these qualifications after 40, and among those I heard from who have done so were a former clerk in a leather factory, a housewife, a retired Royal Navy officer, and a local government official.

BUILDING TRADES

It is possible to make a late start in most of the trades involved in the building industry, but you are likely to need relevant experience or qualifications or both to be taken on by an employer. However, there is nothing to stop you becoming self-employed as, say, a decorator, carpenter or plumber, if you have acquired a sufficient level of competence in your chosen speciality, perhaps through years as a DIY enthusiast. Late career changers often start with commissions from relatives and friends, and expand from there. Much of the business is likely to come through personal recommendations, perhaps backed up with a modest amount of advertising, for example in the *Yellow Pages* and through cards placed in local shop windows. There may also be opportunities for sub-contracting work with other firms.

In most of these occupations it pays to be fairly fit, have a head for heights and, in plumbing at least, not to be too squeamish! Once the enterprise is established a good living can be made, though of course business can fluctuate according to economic conditions.

If you want to hone your skills or acquire new ones, a variety of City and Guilds, BTEC, HNC and HND courses are available at local colleges. The Construction Industry Training Board is a useful source of information.

ENGINEERING

The engineering profession is anxious to attract more high calibre candidates, including suitably experienced mature entrants, and has worked hard in recent years to cast off an image of being one of the less exciting or rewarding professions.

The many branches of the profession offer an extremely wide range of challenging career opportunities. The outlook for late entrants depends on background and training, and also on the particular branch of engineering they wish to enter. The main career levels are chartered engineer, for which a degree iş necessary, incorporated engineer, engineering technician and craftsperson, and operator.

Most of the professional engineering institutions publish their own requirements for membership, but liaise closely with each other through the Engineering Council.

A variety of courses is available full-time or part-time at further and higher education institutions, and the Engineering Careers Information Service (ECIS) will be glad to send literature and answer your queries. Several of the professional institutions also issue career guides, and the ECIS will put you in touch with any in which you are specifically interested.

CHECK LIST

- Most of the professions discussed in this chapter offer opportunities for self-employment.

- If the length of training needed to enter a profession at the higher level is off-putting, there is scope to train in the same field at a lower level of entry.

- Consider one of the many branches of engineering; some courses are available part-time.

5

Classes and Culture

TEACHING

Secondary and primary teaching

Teaching is one of the most welcoming of the professions for the over-40s, especially for those who already have a degree in a subject where there are staff shortages in some areas, such as physics, mathematics, modern languages, and craft, design and technology.

Degree holders can apply to take a one year postgraduate certificate in education (PGCE), which for those wanting to teach in secondary schools will be two-thirds classroom based. A distance learning PGCE is being developed by the Open University.

The industrial and commercial experience of mature candidates is highly valued and an increasingly common option for such entrants is the *licensed teacher scheme*. This provides for school-based training leading to qualified teacher status after an average of about two years. Check with your local education authority or your nearest higher education institution whether the scheme is operative in your area.

Minimum entry requirements for teacher training are laid down by the Department of Education and the Scottish and Northern Ireland departments. All applicants have to demonstrate an acceptable level of competence in English language and mathematics.

Education has undergone wide-ranging changes in organisation and content in recent years and middle-agers entering teaching today are likely to find schools very different places from those in which they were taught. However, the essential qualities needed by a teacher have probably changed little. In the view of the Department of Education they include:

- the ability to think fast on your feet;
- an enquiring mind;
- patience;
- flexibility;
- good communication skills; and
- strong self-motivation.

The Department stresses that 'Mature entrants have much to offer the teaching profession — and much to gain from it.'

This is how some middle-agers found their transition to teaching:

My confidence was dented on several occasions by comments from various people, including the family doctor and local head teacher, that I was rather old to be embarking on a career in education. I had left work with no qualifications and made no effort to study until starting a night class at 40. At the college of education I often had to study well into the night to keep up with the work, particularly in years one and two. Remembering all the doubts and worries I had at the outset, the day I discovered that I had not only qualified but obtained a distinction was the happiest day of my life. (*Scottish primary school headmaster; former coal miner*)

The other 20 or so students on my course were female and mostly young, so sometimes I felt awkward, as for instance in the drama sessions. In any case I am a rather reserved person. I enjoyed the music element of the course and was able to bring to my study many years of practice in keyboard skills. I found the course difficult at times and had to retake two of the second year examinations. (*BEd graduate in creative arts, Leeds Metropolitan University; former insurance salesman*)

The young students are real friends, who help me along. Often I feel 18 and act 18. I have been to discos, the theatre, the lot. I suppose my real strength is that I love children and young people. (*BA student in education, St. Mary's College, Twickenham; member of religious community*)

The former occupations of other contributors included train driver, university lecturer, youth worker, mining engineer, postman, secretary, sales manager, self-employed builder, and community education officer.

To find out more about the opportunities in teaching, ask the TASC Publicity Unit at the Department of Education to send you their latest literature.

Nursery nursing
For those who enjoy working with younger children, the nursery nursing profession offers a variety of opportunities, including employment on classroom duties in primary schools and work in day nurseries, family centres and hospitals.

The normal qualification route is through a two year full-time course or three year part-time course leading to the certificate awarded by the National Nursery Examination Board (NNEB). Training is available at over 170 colleges around the country, some of which have courses specially geared to the needs of older students.

Enid, a former playgroup leader who completed her training at 50, told me, 'It was a busy though sometimes stressful course, but a wonderful two years in which I learned a lot about children and people in general. I was advised by my tutors that I would be best suited to working among under-privileged children. They respond well and gain confidence in my care, which is a tremendous thrill to me. It is very rewarding work and being older means you are more relaxed.'

Patricia, who previously worked as a school meals lady and playgroup supervisor, trained as a nursery nurse because she wanted a more challenging and better paid job. She also saw her new career as a stepping stone to furthering her career, possibly as an infant teacher.

Playgroup organiser

If you have a suitable room at home or can hire a local hall, you could consider setting up a pre-school playgroup. You would need to fulfil certain health and safety criteria with regard to premises and the number of children in the group. Your local authority can advise on the requirements.

You do not require any formal qualifications, though an appropriate training course would be helpful, as would previous experience of working with children.

Further and higher education

The further and higher education sector is a fruitful area of opportunity for middle-aged career changers, and several contributors with backgrounds in management and office work reported finding teaching posts in business studies and commercial subjects. Others have found satisfying teaching work with the Youth Training Scheme and Employment Training courses, basic literacy and numeracy skills coaching for adults, and evening classes.

There is no statutory requirement for teachers in this sector to possess a professional teaching qualification, but they are normally expected to have recognised credentials in the subject being taught and relevant professional, industrial or business experience. There is a growing trend for further education teachers to acquire a teaching qualification, and this is likely to intensify under the single European market.

Correspondence colleges
For those with degrees or professional qualifications who don't necessarily want to work full time, there are potential teaching opportunities as tutors with one of the numerous correspondence colleges operating in the UK. A list of the colleges can be obtained from the Council for the Accreditation of British Correspondence Colleges. If the ones you contact don't have an immediate vacancy they may put you on their waiting lists; most of the colleges maintain such lists.

MEDIA AND COMMUNICATIONS

Journalism
This is a profession in which maturity, reliability and contacts can be valuable assets, and it seems that the outlook for older would-be entrants has been improving.

The National Council for the Training of Journalists (NCTJ), which runs courses for reporters and press photographers, advised that in recent years a number of editors had shown increasing interest in taking on recruits of more mature years.

A newspaper group in the south-east told me that it had started taking trainees in their forties and fifties because younger journalists often tended to move on as soon as they were trained. The group has found that its mature entrants not only brought much local knowledge, but extra bonuses such as good attendance and health records, and their example has encouraged better performance from their younger colleagues.

To take an NCTJ course it is necessary first to find a place on the staff of a newspaper. Some newspaper groups run their own NCTJ approved training programmes, and it is possible to do a one year full-time course at one of several colleges around the country followed by 18 months on-the-job training.

A pre-entry course for journalism aimed principally at mature students is run by Cornwall College at Redruth. Pauline, a former ships' stewardess who began the course at 45, told me she was finding it hard work, especially the retention of information on such subjects as law and public administration, and building up speed in Teeline shorthand. She advised others taking the course to 'prepare yourself to devote every waking minute to it, and tell friends and family that you are going to ignore their letters and offers of social gatherings for one year.'

While the most promising area of entry to journalism appears to be local newspapers, the periodical press is also worth exploring. Maggie, a Kent school teacher, disillusioned with overwork, low pay and poor morale in teaching, found a post at the age of 45 in the editorial department of a jewellery trade magazine. The work involved gathering stories, dealing with typesetters, helping with page layouts and passing them for press. Maggie, who had worked her way up to become deputy editor, told me, 'I work less hours than I did in teaching, I am paid more, there are more perks, and I feel less stressed. I wish I had made the change years ago.'

A pre-entry course for journalists in the periodicals industry is run under the auspices of the Periodicals Training Council.

See also the section on Creative Writing, chapter 11.

Public relations

Most of the over-40s who enter the public relations business have a background in a related field, such as journalism, marketing or advertising. Specialist knowledge in other areas can also sometimes be a passport into PR, as, for example, ex-members of Parliament who are taken on by firms specialising in political lobbying.

There is no universally agreed definition of 'public relations' and practitioners' titles may include words such as 'press', 'communications', 'public affairs', 'public information', and so on. Some who consider themselves PR professionals do little more than write press releases about their clients' or employer's latest products, while others are high powered policy advisers to the captains of industry. Between these two extremes a wide range of activities are carried out in the cause of what the Institute of Public Relations has defined as 'the planned and sustained effort to establish and maintain goodwill and mutual understanding between an organisation and its publics.'

The fast growth of the public relations industry in recent years has inspired the establishment of an increasing number of degree and diploma courses in PR and related subjects, but the most widely followed training courses are those set by the Communications, Advertising and Marketing Foundation (CAM). These are staged at a number of colleges around the country, and can be followed part-time.

Advertising

No formal qualifications are needed to work for an advertising agency, but previous relevant experience is necessary for late

starters. If you don't have this the best place to try and get it is in a
small agency, which is more likely to provide a broad grounding,
than a larger 'shop' where there is greater specialisation and
segmentation of functions.

However, even with personal connections or with experience in
some related field like marketing or public relations, you won't find
it easy to get your foot in the advertising door. You could strengthen
your credentials and your know-how by taking a CAM course,
either at evening class or by correspondence. Bear in mind, though,
that advertising, especially in the larger agencies, is a pressurised,
competitive business with a high staff turnover. Some of its
brightest stars move out or burn out by middle age.

While advertising agencies may be regarded as the sharp end of
the business, there are also opportunities for those with appropriate
skills to work in the advertising departments of business of all kinds,
or for suppliers of advertising services, such as commercial film
studios and market research agencies.

Publishing

Competition for jobs in publishing is keen, but some determined
middle-aged career changers nevertheless manage to find places.

Joy, a publishing consultant who spent many years working for
major imprints such as Penguin, Nelson and Cassell, advised, 'This
is one of the careers you can enter in mid-life. Don't be discouraged
by the difficulty of getting started. A friend of mine applied for 43
jobs before she got her first one. Be persistent to the point of bloody
mindedness. It's wonderful if you succeed. Don't try unless you
have a good standard of literacy, a wide general knowledge and/or
competence in one specific discipline, and, most important, a
passionate love of books. Realise you have an enormous amount to
learn. Secretarial skills are valuable.'

A former teacher of English and linguistics, Gwyneth, got her
start in publishing as a part-time lexicographer with a firm
producing materials for the teaching of English as a foreign or
second language. She did so well that she eventually became
editorial director with complete day-to-day control of the company.
One of the initial problems, she said, was 'having enough self-
confidence to believe you can be successful in a new career,
especially when working with people much younger than yourself
who are already experienced.'

While those who start their own publishing ventures in middle
age are often refugees from other publishing houses or writers

determined to get their own work into print, the profession also has room for others with less directly relevant experience.

Hilary, formerly an occupational therapist, told me how she started producing guide books as a hobby, but then found it took so much of her time and energy she decided to become a full-time publisher. The business grew and she had to take on a full-time assistant and a part-timer as well as using freelance help. A distribution company handles her sales in Britain while sales to other countries are invoiced and despatched 'in-house'. She said her inexperience in business matters led to some cash flow problems and a fairly expensive process of trial and error. There had been offers to merge or be taken over, but she was not considering them yet. 'Perhaps in a few years I may be tempted,' she said. Her advice to other newcomers to independent publishing: 'Choose a subject that you know, and specialise. Join the Independent Publishers Guild. Do not expect to make much money.'

Films and television
Without some previous relevant experience it is difficult to break into the film and television industries, or to find a place on a professional training course.

The National Film and Television School at Beaconsfield, Buckinghamshire, sets no formal age limits for entry to its professional training course, which takes up to three years, but advises that most successful candidates are in their twenties.

There was little encouragement either from the London International Film School. The principal told me that in the case of mature applicants, particularly those in their thirties and older, he 'always take great pains to emphasise the highly competitive, and in the main, freelance, nature of the film and TV industries.' He said the industries had changed fundamentally in the last 10 or 15 years and are essentially young people's industries.

For those still determined to try their luck, some higher education institutions offer courses in film and television skills, and workshops are run by a number of other organisations. A list of courses is available from the British Film Institute (price £2.90 plus 30p p&p).

Video production
There has been a rapid growth in the use of videos for education, training and promotional purposes during the past decade. Many independent companies have been formed by people from the television and film world, but others have been set up by men and

women from unrelated fields.

Tony, who accepted early retirement from his teaching job at a West Midlands school because rolls were falling, established a production company to capitalise on experience gained making video films during the latter part of his teaching career. Since forming his company he has produced videos for such clients as the Royal Air Force, Marks and Spencer, the Royal Society for the Prevention of Accidents and local companies.

A qualified glider pilot, Tony specialises in aerial video films and handles production projects from initial consultation through scripting, shooting and editing. 'I find that being my own master, planning my own time and having to sell my abilities on an open market is in many ways far more rewarding than my previous career,' he told me. 'Old skills have been honed and new ones developed (I am now computer semi-literate!).'

Photography

Given some amateur experience, a little creative flair, good eyesight, and a willingness to work hard and seek out assignments, there are opportunities for the late starter to break into the ranks of paid photographers.

One way of getting some on-the-job training is to build up a portfolio of work and offer your services to a local photographic firm covering weddings, school groups, etc. You could also try your hand at some speculative freelance work for the local press at, for example, fêtes, parades and other local events. As your skills and reputation grow, you could try your luck in more lucrative fields, such as advertising, medical or scientific photography, but standards are very high and competition fierce.

For those with little or no technical background in photography a vocational course at a further educational college could be a wise move at the outset. A helpful link with the professionals can be forged by obtaining affiliate membership of the British Institute of Professional Photography. Among other things Institute membership entitles you to the use of its advisory service and receipt of its magazine, *The Photographer*, a useful source of second-hand and discounted equipment, as well as job vacancies.

POLITICS

Given a reasonably thick skin, not too many skeletons in the cupboard, and no hang-ups about job security, you could explore the possibilities of getting yourself nominated to run for elective office for local government, the House of Commons, or even the European Parliament.

At a local level it's a part-time, expenses only kind of job, but for Westminster and Europe, where the pay and perks are good, you will be up against fierce competition for selection as a candidate. Your maturity and experience might work in your favour, however; there is always a sizeable contingent of over-40s in the batch of new MPs entering Parliament at each general election. In the 1992 contest all but 81 of the 651 MPs elected were over 40. The intake included award-winning actress Glenda Jackson, who won Hampstead for Labour at the age of 55. Several members of the present cabinet were over 40 when they entered Parliament, as was the Liberal Democrat leader Paddy Ashdown.

Those who would like to be professionally involved in politics without facing the regular spotlight of publicity could explore the possibility of becoming a political agent for one of the major parties. The Conservatives have an upper age limit of 48 for recruits to this work. Contact the nearest office or the central headquarters of your favourite political party and ask for information.

CAREERS WITH LANGUAGES

Translator/interpreter

Your level of fluency and competence in one or more foreign languages will be more important than your age if you are looking for an opportunity to employ your linguistic skills as a translator or interpreter. Translators can work from home and the investment need only be modest, ie a typewriter and some good dictionaries and reference books. Be prepared, though, for stiff competition from native speakers of the major European languages.

Working as a freelance professional interpreter can involve a lot of travel to international meetings and conferences. You would be well advised to take an interpreter's course — the one at the University of Central London is highly regarded — and join the *Association des Interpretes de Conferences*.

The Institute of Linguists sets examinations in translation and interpreting, which can be prepared for by part-time or correspondence study.

TEFL

Teaching English as a foreign language (TEFL) to foreign students is a popular choice for career changers. You do not need to speak the language of the people you are teaching, though language skills and previous teaching experience are useful.

The first step is to take a recognised training course – the Royal Society of Arts (RSA) preliminary certificate can be completed in a month of full-time study — with a reputable training organisation, such as International House, the largest independent British-based organisation for teaching English.

The demand for English instruction in the UK and around the world has been growing rapidly in recent years, and the columns of vacancies in the press for TEFL teachers suggest there are plenty of openings. However, the marketing director of International House warned that the terms and conditions of employment can tend to discriminate against older candidates. Salaries are not sufficient for someone to support dependents, such as children or a non-employed spouse. There is strong competition for UK-based jobs and salaries in the private language schools, the biggest UK employers, do not compare favourably with industry and the public sector.

The Association of Recognised English Language Schools-Federation of English Language Course Organisations (ARELS-FELCO) will send you a list of recognised schools.

LIBRARIES

Librarian
Maturity and experience are helpful assets for a professional librarian, as are such qualities as thoroughness and patience. It is also important to be able to relate to clients and understand their information needs, and modern librarians take pride in their management skills and ability to exploit new technology.

In recent years there has been an increase in the number of higher education institutions offering part-time courses in librarianship and information studies to meet the needs of mature entrants whose circumstances prevent them for studying full-time. Other courses include those leading to the City and Guilds librarian and information assistant's certificate.

Archivist
There is not a vast field of opportunity for late starters in this field, but one worth exploring if you are interested in the past, enjoy working with historical materials, and maintaining current records for future use.

Employers may include local or central government, private companies, professional and educational institutions, and many other types of organisations. You will need a good degree, usually in history, English, Latin or another classical language.

MUSEUMS

'Museum work provides an enormously enjoyable and satisfying career. Hugely varied and attracting a wide variety of people, the museum "business" is booming. Some 70 million visits are made every year to museums, and museums combine as nothing else does the virtues of education and entertainment.' So says the Museum Association, but goes on to warn that the principal drawback to most museum jobs is that they are poorly paid, and job security is no longer guaranteed. Nevertheless competition remains intense for openings, especially for curator posts. While curators, who are normally required to have degrees, are responsible for a museum's collections, other staff carry out vital work in such areas as research, conservation, education, design, taxidermy, photography, sales, marketing, public relations, management and finance.

No upper age limits are laid down for entry to museum work, but late starters will normally be expected to have relevant experience and qualifications.

(See also the section on the leisure industry, chapter 9.)

ARCHAEOLOGY

Do you have a fascination with fossils, relics, and the remains of ancient civilisations? Would you like to spend your time uncovering them at sites around the globe? Your ambition may be achievable, but the rewards are unlikely to be of the financial kind, and the work can be hard, manual, often dirty, and carried out in all kinds of climatic conditions. Fares are not usually paid for travel to sites, though food and accommodation and sometimes even a little pocket money may be provided.

Probably your best strategy is to immerse yourself in the literature of the subject, take some of the many part-time courses available (study for a degree or diploma if you want to go the whole hog), join your local archaeological society, find out who's digging what and where, and offer your services as a well-informed amateur.

You will probably want to try some digs in the UK before looking further afield. The Council for British Archaeology publishes information about digs in this country, and the *Archaeology Abroad* bulletin, issued three times a year, contains information on digs at overseas sites.

The honorary secretary of *Archaeology Abroad* offered this advice: 'Accommodation on sites is usually on campsites, and the work is manual and often heavy. I "dug" for several years and have to admit to giving it up for less strenuous occupations when I reached 40. However there are several "over-40s" who dig for pleasure in their spare time, usually with their county units or local society. Unfortunately paid archaeological jobs are few and far between.'

There is intense competition among the professionals for the limited number of full-time jobs that become available in universities, research organisations and museums.

6

Healers and Carers

HEALTH PROFESSIONS

The health care professions offer the over-40s a variety of satisfying, though often not lucrative career opportunities.

While maturity and life experience may be seen as useful attributes in many branches of health work, applicants have to demonstrate that they have the capacity to cope with the training, and the necessary aptitudes and qualities to handle the kind of responsibilities that lie at the end of it. The chances of landing a place in a medical or dental school may be remote, but the prognosis is more hopeful in a number of other health occupations, including the many specialities in the burgeoning field of complementary or alternative medicine.

For convenient reference the entries in this section are broadly divided into those professions which operate within the National Health Service as well as in the private sector, followed by some of the more popular branches of complementary medicine.

Orthodox health care

Ambulance Service

Recruitment after the age of 45 is unlikely, except as a care assistant, whose main duties involve transporting infirm and elderly patients to and from hospitals and day centres. For this work men and women may be accepted up to 55. A clean driving licence is needed.

Contact your local health authority or ambulance station (addresses can be found in the phone book) for more information.

Audiology

This speciality offers mature career changers a number of fascinating options, but for many of them you need a degree, sometimes a medical qualification, before being able to take the specialised training involved. The opportunities range from audiological scientist and otolaryngologist to speech therapist and teacher of the deaf.

Chiropody

Most of the schools of chiropody consider mature applicants on their merits, and all have their own entry requirements. The Society of Chiropodists will provide a list of recognised schools.

Completion of a three year diploma course at a recognised school is a prerequisite to qualifying for state registration. This enables you to work in the National Health Service or, if you prefer, as a private practitioner. Private practice offers the opportunity of more flexible hours and potentially higher earnings.

Chiropody is a very suitable career for mature people with an interest in biology, according to Jacqueline, a former part-time teacher and mother of six, who qualified as a state registered chiropodist at the Matthew Boulton Technical College in Birmingham at the age of 44. 'I found the course tougher than I expected,' she said, 'It was multi-disciplinary and required a wide range of knowledge. The subjects included anatomy, pharmacology, pathology, microbiology, therapeutics, medicine, surgery and biomechanics. The course was very structured with little free time.' Jacqueline, a science graduate from Birmingham University, now teaches at a school of chiropody.

Joan, a mother of three and former laboratory assistant who left school at 16 with four O levels, turned to chiropody as an adult because she 'wanted a career with skill and status to do with helping people.' After graduation from the School of Chiropody at Nene College, Northampton, she went into private practice. 'It is frightening to leave the cocoon and security of college for the unknown, especially when not protected by the National Health Service,' said Joan, 'but I am a good chiropodist, patients feel comfortable with me, so I know it's just a matter of getting on and doing it.'

Dentistry

While applications from the over-40s to train as dentists are unlikely to get past the first sift by admission officers, there are a number of opportunities for older candidates in allied occupations.

Dental therapists, whose tasks include simple fillings, extraction of deciduous teeth, and scaling and polishing, take a two year course; dental hygienists, who also scale and polish, and give instruction on dental hygiene, study for one year; dental technicians, who make dentures, can train on the job and attend part-time courses or train full-time for three years. Dental surgery assistants and receptionists commonly train on the job, but part-time or full-time courses are available and staff can qualify for the National Certificate for Dental Surgery Assistants.

Dietetics
The skills of the dietician are in demand in many areas, including hospitals, government departments, the community, food production, retailing, research and sport.

While no formal barriers exist to 40-plus entrants, the normal route to statutory registration is a four-year course in nutrition or dietetics. It is possible, however, for graduates in other disciplines with sufficient emphasis on human biochemistry and physiology to do a two year post-graduate diploma course instead.

Health Service management
There is no formal upper age limit for non-medical management recruits to the National Health Service. The work involves general management and co-ordination of hospital medical and nursing services. Previous relevant expertise is valuable, as are qualifications in such areas as accountancy, personnel work, purchasing and supply, and information technology.

Applications from mature men and women are also welcomed for clerical jobs and posts such as receptionists and admissions and ward clerks. Check with the personnel office at your local health authority.

Homeopathy
The approach of the homeopath is to treat the whole patient rather than particular symptoms. Natural remedies are used to trigger the body's own healing powers. The system is practised with animals as well as people.

Homeopathy is available under the NHS though it is practised by only a minority of doctors. Training as a homeopath provides the doctor or veterinary surgeon with an opportunity not so much to change his or her career but to alter its emphasis.

Medicine
If your ambition is to become a doctor and you are over 30, don't expect much encouragement from most British medical schools. Although they may not publish formal upper age limits for entry, their admissions policies are significantly influenced by such factors as the considerable cost to the taxpayer of medical training, the high demand for places from younger applicants, and the number of

years that the newly qualified doctor is likely to be able to give to the health service. A medical course normally takes five or six years, followed by a qualifying year, and further training is required to work in many areas of medicine. Nevertheless, I have heard from several doctors who were in their forties when they qualified.

Martha, a former nurse whose experience includes several years in Morocco, qualified in France at the age of 47 after previously being turned down by several British medical schools. She took her course at a university in Toulouse, where she did not have to pay fees except for a small registration charge. 'Apart from doing everything in French, I had to learn endless formulae, which I thought would be my downfall,' she said. 'But it wasn't, and I scraped through. From copying other people's notes in the first year, people were soon copying mine.' After qualifying she returned to Britain and put her skills at the disposal of the National Health Service, working in the field of geriatrics and psychiatry.

Ruth, a former English teacher at a comprehensive school, who graduated from a London medical school in her fortieth year and subsequently went into general practice, felt strongly about the value of changing jobs in mid-life. 'I was influenced by my mother who got her degree at 50 and changed from a secretary to a teacher,' she said. 'There are always Jeremiahs who put obstacles of doubt in one's way and tell you no-one will offer you a place/give you a job etc., but my experience was that, in the long run, it was surprisingly easy; in many ways my age and experience has proved an asset rather than a hindrance and I have got exactly the jobs I wanted so far — and that in a conservative profession like medicine.'

Other respondents who became medical practitioners in their forties were a former engineering lecturer, a housing manager and a general practitioner's wife.

Medical secretary
Mature people with relevant experience are usually welcome candidates for jobs as secretaries or administrators in medical practices and hospitals.

On-the-job training is given, and courses may be taken at local further education colleges to obtain qualifications from the Association of Medical Secretaries, Practice Administrators and Receptionists. Normal entry requirements for the Association's courses may be waived for mature applicants if they have appropriate experience in the health field or possess shorthand and typing skills.

Nursing

Applications from men and women over 40 are encouraged by many nurse training schools, and a few will consider candidates over 50. The nurses' professional body, the Royal College of Nursing (RCN), recognises the value of 'life experience' that mature men and women bring with them, and believes that more of them must be drawn into the profession. A report on manpower produced for the RCN stated, 'A nurse who trains at the age of 40 still has many years of valuable service ahead and many years of past experience to draw on.' At present about 90 per cent of nurses are women, and the profession is keen to attract more male applicants.

Neither your sex nor your maturity alone, however, will be enough to win you a place on a nursing course; your background and personality will obviously be important factors, as will evidence of your capacity for study.

There are two levels of qualification — Enrolled Nurse (EN), which involves a two year course (18 months in Scotland) and Registered General Nurse (RGN), which takes three years.

For Alexandra, a former secretary, nursing was what she had always wanted to do, but she waited to begin her studies until her youngest son started school. Although having 'little academic pedigree', she felt that the important qualities she brought to her new career were common sense, understanding of life and a rapport with fellow human beings. She graduated at 43 as an RGN and believes that the medical knowledge she gained was 'a bonus to my life', adding, 'I feel extremely worthwhile at a time when many women feel lost.'

Most married students feel the strains of balancing the busy schedule of nursing training and study with family and domestic responsibilities. Susan, a 42-year-old RGN student in the first year of her course, told me, 'I am in a permanent state of exhaustion. I come home, collapse in a chair, and go to bed early. There isn't much of a life outside nursing at the moment.'

One of the profession's male recruits, John, formerly a buyer with an agricultural feed company who began his nursing studies at the age of 43, settled easily into what has traditionally been regarded as a predominantly female preserve. 'Relations with other students, staff and tutors have not caused me any problems, he said, 'and I have found I have enjoyed aspects of nursing I had not thought possible, such as working in a geriatric ward. I have never been an idealist, and do not have the hang-ups about the shortcomings of the system and its practices that the younger ones do, and so perhaps I avoid most of the rough patches. Twenty years attendance at the university of life is a very valuable if intangible asset.'

For nurses over 40 who wish to specialise in areas such as midwifery or health visiting, their age is no bar to taking the necessary additional training. There are also opportunities, with no specified upper age limit, for mature men and women without nursing training to work as nursing auxiliaries or assistants, and porters. Check with your local hospitals for vacancies.

Occupational therapy

Occupational therapists are employed mainly by the NHS and local authority social services, working in hospitals, special centres and in the homes of handicapped people. They employ a variety of activities and techniques to treat people with physical or mental problems, whether temporary or permanent, to help them cope with everyday life.

The training for this profession is fairly strenuous and the job is demanding. It may not be a suitable choice for anyone with physical difficulties.

For mature applicants who can show evidence of recent academic study and scientific ability, schools of occupational therapy may waive their normal educational entry requirements. Experience in some branch of nursing or as a physiotherapist can reduce the length of training, which is normally three years full-time. The diploma of the British Association of Occupational Therapists provides qualification for state registration, and enables the holder to work in the NHS or the private sector.

Lesley, a former cook/manageress who graduated from the Glasgow School of Occupational Therapy in her forties, told me, 'Occupational therapy appealed to me because of the nature of the work and the concept behind the way the treatment is given to patients; that is the use of activity in a practical sense to aid recovery. On placements working in hospitals occasionally more was expected of you than of younger students, and supervisors may have been a little apprehensive at having an older person to supervise, but in general I was treated like any other student.'

It is also possible to work as an occupational therapist's helper. No formal qualifications are required, but you need to be fit and strong to cope with lifting and moving patients.

Optical work

If you have your eyes on a career in optical work, two of the specialisms to consider are those of optometrist (also known as an opthalmic optician), who examines eyes, tests sight and prescribes spectacles or contact lenses, and the dispensing optician, who fits and supplies lenses and contact lenses prescribed by the optometrist or opthalmic medical practitioner. Many optometrists also supplement their income by selling spectacles and other optical appliances. Since the deregulation of the selling of spectacles the competition for business has become increasingly fierce, especially among the larger retail outlets.

Both optometrists and dispensing opticians have to be registered with the General Optical Council before they can practise. The qualifying procedure for optometrists involves a three year degree course, a pre-registration year working with a qualified member of the profession, and the passing of a professional examination. Dispensing opticians follow a shorter training programme.

Pharmacy

'Although retraining as a pharmacist is a lengthy process, it is a viable mid-career change of direction; there are no age restrictions on gaining a place at a school of pharmacy, or on obtaining a position as either a pre-registration or a registered pharmacist.' That is the message from the pharmacists' professional body, the Royal Pharmaceutical Society of Great Britain.

Apart from their familiar community role in the chemist's shop, career opportunities for pharmacists also exist in hospitals, industry and research.

Qualification involves a three year degree course followed by a year's paid practical training. In the case of mature applicants the schools of pharmacy may consider some relaxation in the normal entry requirements.

Those deterred by the length of full-time training involved in qualifying as a pharmacist might prefer to consider training as a pharmacy technician, and working under the supervision of a pharmacist preparing and dispensing medicines and handling related tasks. This would involve obtaining a position with a pharmacist and studying on a day-release or correspondence basis. More information about this option can be obtained from the National Pharmaceutical Association.

Physiotherapy

In recent years physiotherapy training schools have adopted a more flexible and sympathetic policy towards applicants over 40. As the principal of one of the schools told me, 'I am convinced that they have much to offer.'

Qualifying as a chartered physiotherapist involves a three or four year full-time course. Most practitioners work in NHS hospitals, but there are also opportunities in private hospitals and practices, sports centres, large companies, educational institutions and community health centres. The demand for the services of physiotherapists is growing, especially in the private sector.

Opportunities also exist to work as a physiotherapist's assistant and for this work no formal qualifications are required.

If you are attracted to this career, try to arrange a visit to the physiotherapy department of a hospital in your area to get an idea of the range of work involved.

Psychology
A degree course of three of more years is normally a necessary preliminary to a career as a psychologist. Mature entrants are welcome on the courses and entry requirements may be relaxed for them.

The main fields of specialisation are educational, clinical or occupational psychology.

Psychotherapy
The maturity and varied life experience which they can bring to the work make psychotherapy a particularly suitable occupation for middle-aged career changers. Much of the work involves listening to the problems of patients, and the psychotherapist needs not only a high level of professional know-how, but patience, concentration and observational skills.

To be admitted to a training course with the British Association of Psychotherapists (BAP) you need a degree in medicine, psychology or social science, or a relevant professional qualification. Some experience of working with disturbed people in a psychotherapeutic capacity is also required. For the Association's Freudian training course the upper age limit is normally 45 and for the Jungian course 50, though these may be varied in exceptional circumstances.

The courses last at least three years (four years for child psychotherapy), during which the students themselves are expected to undergo an extended period of therapy with an approved therapist.

Jane, a former computer programmer who took the Freudian course, beginning aged 42, told me, 'It's very absorbing and rather takes over one's life, especially as it entails training analysis/therapy three times a week. Because of the requirement that candidates be analysed the course is expensive. I find it very satisfying work, and it is also a field which enables one to meet a community of like minded people both within the training organisation and in the field. This refers to London, however, and I know that it is not true in many/most other places, where loneliness can be a problem. Study carefully the differences between the training programmes to choose the right one for you.'

The Jungian stream was chosen by Cleone, a former army nursing sister and marriage guidance counsellor, who started her BAP training at 49. 'To pay for the training I became a staff nurse in a hospital psychiatric unit two days a week,' she said. 'I have had a private practice three days a week since I qualified as an associate of the BAP (I became a full member three years later). I describe myself as a late developer, and I am now in my final year of a BA degree with the Open University.'

(See also 'Hypnotherapy' on page 76).

Radiography
To qualify for state registration as a radiographer you have to take a three year course and pass examinations set by the College of Radiographers. The College does not set a formal upper age limit for entry to training, but policy varies between schools and some draw the line at 45.

Libby, a former history teacher who graduated from the Stoke-on-Trent School of Radiography in her early forties, told me, 'Mature students are accepted pretty naturally these days, and in my experience are made extremely welcome.' She found the course 'a fascinating combination of theory and practice' and 'a great opportunity for anyone arts-based to find out a bit about science.' After qualification she progressed to become a senior therapy radiographer employed by the Medical Research Council and is involved in the planning and execution of treatments, mainly for malignant disease. 'I still find the theoretical side very interesting, but people with cancer can be very special,' she said. 'The human contact can be humbling, desperately sad, happy, difficult. You find a great sense of perspective and proportion, and you feel a bit of use — sometimes! Surprising how much humour there is in the day. You can't take on too much; you have to watch emotional involvement, and keep it under control. Working with potentially lethal radiation is a responsibility, and making mistakes is *not* fun.'

Complementary medicine
The many therapies and treatment systems which comprise what is

variously referred to as complementary, alternative, fringe or natural medicine have long provided a fruitful area of second careers for the over 40s.

Most practitioners prefer the term complementary medicine because they feel this best describes their relationship to orthodox medicine. Some of the complementary therapies have been around in one form or another for centuries, and a number are enjoying a significant growth in popularity. Part of their appeal is that they offer treatment alternatives to the surgical procedures and drug regimes associated with conventional medicine. Sometimes 'natural' treatments are sought after orthodox methods have proved unsuccessful. The techniques employed may involve, among other things, the use of small needles, magnets, oils, salts, manipulation of joints, dietary management, and massage.

Some of the specialisms, such as acupuncture, herbalism and osteopathy, are well known while others are much less familiar. The different treatment systems have achieved varying degrees of respectability in the eyes of orthodox medical practitioners, but some are still regarded as dubious, eccentric, or worse, and the cause of the many dedicated and reputable complementary therapists has sometimes been damaged by the activities of a minority of unprincipled operators attracted to the field by the absence of statutory regulation and the lure of easy money.

Most of the establishments which train practitioners in the various branches of complementary medicine welcome applications from mature candidates, and some courses qualify for local authority discretionary grants.

Acupuncture
This ancient Chinese therapy, widely practised around the world, treats the cause and symptoms of illness by inserting specially made fine needles at specific points in the body. The method is also used to induce anaesthesia.

Some middle-agers who train as acupuncturists come from other orthodox or alternative medical fields while others have no previous background in a healing profession. The British College of Acupuncture in London runs courses for registered members of the medical, dental, nursing and other health care professions; the College for Traditional Chinese Acupuncture (CTCA) at Leamington Spa and the London School of Acupuncture and Traditional Chinese Medicine (LSATCM) accept applicants from other backgrounds.

The CTCA advised that applicants are considered on merit regardless of age. Where they do not meet the standard academic entry requirements, professional qualifications and work experience are taken into account. 'One of the most important qualifications for admission,' the college stated, 'is a sincere, caring attitude and a willingness to grow internally and learn an approach which will probably be completely new.'

The registrar of the LSATCM told me 'The founders of this college all came to acupuncture as a career change, as do the bulk of our students.'

Aromatherapy
Practitioners use oils extracted from plants to massage the face and body to relieve ailments and improve health. Some of the oils may also be taken internally.

Chiropractic
The chiropractor uses manipulation of the spine and other joints to treat disorders affecting the nervous system.

To qualify for membership of the professional body, the British Chiropractic Association, you have to complete a four year full-time course at an accredited college. The only such establishment in the UK is the Anglo-European College of Chiropractic in Bournemouth. There are special provisions for mature students who do not meet the normal entry requirements.

The Academic Registrar told me the College had a number of entrants over 40, and the student body ranged in age from 18 to 48. 'Chiropractic lends itself very well to a second career for mature students,' she said. 'It is an obvious advantage in any primary care profession, as far as the patient is concerned, to have maturity.' Although there is no formal upper age limit for the College's course they have found from past experience that those over the age of 50 have considerable difficulty unless they already have a medical/science background, and rarely complete the course.

Herbalism
Medical herbalism, one of the oldest forms of medicine, involves the use of plants and their extracts to treat and prevent illness. It is a popular choice for mature career changers, and both full-time and postal tuition courses are available through training schools in Hailsham, East Sussex, and Tunbridge Wells, Kent.

Recovering from a serious illness with the help of 'natural medicine' after orthodox treatment had failed motivated Nadia, a former antique dealer, to study herbal medicine so that she could apply the same methods to helping others with degenerative diseases. She began a four year full-time training at the School of Herbal Medicine in Tunbridge Wells at the age of 41, and found that her mature years 'served in every way as an advantage.' She said she felt she had found her vocation, and after finishing the course would like eventually to also train in acupuncture, perhaps in China.

Hypnotherapy
This is a specialism in which older candidates are positively welcomed, and the majority of practitioners are believed to be in the 46–55 age group. Practitioners use hypnosis to help patients overcome emotional and relationship difficulties, harmful habits and phobias and other problems, as well as certain physical conditions. It is a form of psychotherapy since it applies psychological principles to the treatment of disorders which are psychological in origin or are exacerbated by psychological factors.

The British Hypnotherapy Association advised that 'experience of life is a great asset in this work' and 'for people contemplating a fresh start in their lives in middle age, hypnotherapy can be particularly suitable, if they have the required integrity, intelligence and education.'

The profession has not always enjoyed the best of reputations and has sometimes been the target of media stories about dubious practitioners and training institutions, but well-run professional training organisations such as the National College of Hypnosis and Psychotherapy at Nelson, Lancashire are doing much to improve the status and image of hypnotherapists. Qualification at the college is achieved through a combination of home study and attendance at weekend training sessions held in London, Cheshire and Glasgow. I heard from several graduates.

Margaret, a former nursery nurse who started her course at 40, told me 'At first my family thought hypnotherapy was a bit crazy, but gave me a lot of encouragement. I found the paperwork very difficult as it was a number of years since I had studied. The language of psychotherapy was totally new to me, but I was interested and enjoyed what I was doing, despite my feelings of inadequacy. It has all been worthwhile. I feel I am getting to know and understand myself, and this is a wonderful experience. I practise part-time, and deal with a lot of habitual problems such as smoking and over-eating. In the past year I have had a number of clients experiencing difficulty coming off tranquilizers.'

A retired senior executive with an electricity board, John began the course aged 64 and qualified for the college diploma in three years. 'I found no difficulty whatever in completing the course,' he said. 'Study and discipline were essential, but I had studied for several lengthy periods of my life, including a law degree completed at 42, and these posed no problems. The course is both academic and practical and was well run. Lectures and demonstrations were interesting both in content and presentation.' In his new profession he works on a part-time basis and said he found the challenge of each new client stimulating.

Other contributors included a former chief housing officer with a local authority and the retired technical director of a major electronics firm.

(See also the section on Psychotherapy on page 72.)

Massage
This familiar system of treatment is one that attracts a number of mature career changers. I heard from two who trained at the Clare Maxwell-Hudson School in London.

Richard, formerly a self-employed maintenance contractor, took a four month course to qualify for the International Therapy Examinations Council (ITEC) certificate in anatomy, physiology and massage, and followed up with an intensive sports massage course. 'The training was first class and very enjoyable,' he said. 'The theory side (anatomy and physiology) was, for me, hard work but very stimulating as I had to get the brain working again after years of more or less operating on "auto pilot".' His practice is growing slowly, but he has found immense job satisfaction. 'Clients come in stressed, hunched up with a painful neck or shoulder, etc.' he said, 'and leave looking and feeling refreshed. Everyone needs massage, the trouble is they don't know it. Half of your job is to get the message across.'

The ITEC certificate was also taken by Gwen, a former university librarian who found the periods spent on placements in two major London hospitals 'particularly rewarding.' Since setting up her practice, she said, her patient list has grown steadily but quite slowly. She sees some patients at home and visits others. 'Don't expect to get a list of clients quickly,' she advised. 'Advertising is not a very wise thing for a woman if working alone. It takes time to become known by word of mouth, and a lot of persistent writing to make oneself known in other ways.'

Nutritional medicine

Older applicants are welcomed for training as nutritional medicine practitioners. The College of Nutritional Medicine, which has clinics in Lancashire, Somerset and London, states that 'Applicants will be considered irrespective of age, nationality, religion, etc. In selecting students the college is particularly interested in the applicant's sensitivity, enthusiasm, open-mindedness and willing- ness to learn.' The college's courses cover both conventional nutrition and alternative nutritional medicine.

Osteopathy

In this system of healing disorders are treated by the use of manipulation, massage and exercise.

Of the three schools accredited by the General Council and Register of Osteopaths, two are located in London and one in Maidstone, Kent. Each of the schools welcomes applications from mature candidates, who may apply for special dispensation if they cannot satisfy standard entry requirements.

Dissatisfaction with his job and a growing interest in physical medicine prompted Howard, a 40-year old executive with a chain of retail stores, to enrol at the British College of Naturopathy and Osteopathy. 'I did consider becoming a doctor,' he said, 'but was led to believe I was too old. The osteopathy course was very intensive and demanded a lot of hard work and dedication, particularly in the last two years.' After graduation he began working for another osteopath, but planned to establish his own practice.

The European School of Osteopathy (ESO) in Maidstone advised that the age range of students on entry was approximately 18–45. Gregory, a former chemical company executive with an MSc degree in chemistry who began his course at the ESO aged 41, told me 'A good scientific background, preferably biologically orientated, is a distinct advantage. The first year can be trying as the student grapples not only with the geography of the body, but also its detailed 3–D functioning, and at the same time learns palpation. This is uncharted territory for most people. My year contains few people who had done any sort of therapy at all.'

Reflexology

The reflexologist diagnoses and treats medical conditions by massaging certain points on the soles of the feet and sometimes the palms of the hands. The purpose is to create a reflex action in another part of the body to improve its functioning and facilitate natural healing.

The training can be undertaken on a part-time basis at weekends at establishments such as Dalamore College of Advanced Reflexology at Radlett, Herts or the British College of Reflexology, Old Harlow, Essex. Two graduates of the latter institution are Joyce, who previously ran a children's wear shop, and James, a former opera coach and producer. She began her training at 58 and he at 71.

Joyce told me 'It was a fascinating course but I had to work hard, especially at the anatomy and physiology, to memorise everything. I followed up by obtaining qualifications in massage and aromatherapy which are compatible. I live in a tiny village and after qualifying needed to build up a practice. I took a short course in public speaking and wrote to local organisations offering my services as a speaker. I find that with recommendations I am now very busy.'

James enjoyed learning the technique and using his hands. 'The studies and experience of giving and receiving reflexology have made me a richer person mentally, physically and spiritually,' he said. 'Ideally entrants to this training should have experienced problems in themselves which they have overcome through holistic healing. I see myself as a cottage industry with just a few patients.'

Shiatsu

This treatment system is related to acupuncture, but instead of needles the therapist applies pressure at specific points around the body to activate innate self-healing mechanisms in the patient.

The British School of Shiatsu-do (*Shiatsu-do* means 'the way of Shiatsu') based in London but with affiliated schools in several other centres, offers part-time courses for those wishing to become practitioners or who simply want to improve their own health. The practitioner diploma takes three years, but the school says its fees are 'kept intentionally low to ensure the availability of Shaitsu-do to all interested.'

Kenneth, a chartered quantity surveyor who was 43 when he earned his Shiatsu-do diploma, now divides his time between his old and new careers. 'I feel a need to balance my lifestyle after 25 years as a surveyor,' he said. 'I also had a desire to be more involved with people and to help. I work at four clinic locations throughout my county. It is a worthwhile career but needs supplementing with other income.'

A former Trinity House pilot, Michael became interested in oriental ideas while working in the Far East and learned Shiatsu to help his son who was suffering from asthma. He took early retirement in his mid-fifties to concentrate on the practice of Shiatsu, and qualified for entry to the Shiatsu Society. He obtains his clients by recommendation, but his service includes going into firms' premises to treat staff members at their work places.

Yoga

This is essentially a self-help system in which practitioners use movements to restore the balance of the body and promote health and spiritual development. The most widely used system in the UK is that taught by the Iyengar Yoga Institute in London, which trains teachers of yoga. The Institute told me 'A number of applicants for our teacher training course are over 40. We do not consider that old!'

Ian, a marine biologist who trained at the Iyengar Institute, attending weekly sessions over two years, said the course was demanding and required strong commitment. He has kept his day job at a London museum, but teaches yoga two nights a week at an adult education centre and twice a week at lunchtime sessions at the museum.

SOCIAL, COMMUNITY AND CHARITABLE WORK

Social work

Social workers are employed mainly by local authorities or voluntary groups, helping others cope with problems associated with such situations as family breakdown, poverty, homelessness, illness, ageing and crime.

As a second career, social work attracts people from a wide variety of backgrounds. The Central Council for Education and Training in Social Work (CCETSW) said the life experience and maturity of older entrants are welcome in the profession. Training is essential and career changers wanting to work as professional social workers now normally take the Diploma in Social Work (DipSW), which replaced the Certificate of Qualification in Social Work (CQSW) as the main standard qualification.

Some courses are designed for older students who, though they may not be asked to meet formal academic requirements, have to convince the selectors of their ability to study at advanced level. Applicants will also be expected to have had some experience related to social work, for example as a voluntary worker in a day centre, hospital, adventure playground, or playgroup. Training in counselling and work with organisations like Relate (formerly the Marriage Guidance Council) or the Samaritans would be valuable.

Jesse, a former dairyman and farmer, earned a CQSW from Newcastle University at the age of 56. He was employed by a local authority and subsequently became a senior social worker in the rehabilitation unit of a psychiatric hospital. 'The main problem I encountered was the change from being the boss to being an employee,' he said. 'I was quite unprepared for some of the attitudes of local government. Forms and more forms were required to do anything. It all took so long and was so cumbersome and frustrating. In the rehabilitation unit, however, innovation, energy and drive were welcomed.'

Some mature students take a degree in sociology, sometimes combined with other subjects such as social policy or administration, education, social and economic history, or industrial studies, before going on to study for the professional qualification in social work. Respondents who followed this route included housewives, secretaries, a nurse, community worker, shop manager, and a bookkeeper.

There are opportunities for older people without formal qualifications to work as social work assistants in the community or a hospital, as home helps assisting the elderly and handicapped, or as wardens of sheltered accommodation for the elderly. The latter job may include accommodation in a house or flat.

Youth and community work

Career opportunities for mature entrants exist in the Youth and Community Service in such locations as clubs and community centres, where the employer may be a local authority, voluntary organisation or youth group, such as the YWCA, YMCA or the National Association of Boys Clubs (NABC). Previous experience in teaching or voluntary work with young people is useful.

Among the workers in this field from whom I heard were three staff members at the NABC, all of whom began their careers there in their forties. Two were ex-Army officers and one a retired police inspector. Each had been involved in education or training in their former occupations and had been eager to continue with that kind of work in civilian life.

Probation Service

The primary aim of the Probation Service is to help offenders stop offending. In pursuit of this objective, the probation officer has to 'advise, assist and befriend' offenders, using social work and other skills.

High on the list of the qualities needed by recruits to the Service, according to the Home Office, are maturity of outlook, emotional maturity, personal stability and an openness to other ideas and opinions. There is no formal upper age limit for entry and each of the 54 probation areas is responsible for its own recruitment policy. The Home Office advised that opportunities for the over-40s 'are likely to vary around the country and over periods of time.'

To work as a probation officer you must hold the DipSW qualification or its equivalent. The Home Office sponsors about 350 candidates a year on recognised courses, and only considers those over 50 in exceptional circumstances, for example where there is a firm undertaking from a probation area to employ the candidate on completion of the course. You can, if you wish, make your own arrangements to study for the diploma.

Counselling

The essential role of a counsellor is to be caring and supportive rather than to give advice. The work involves listening to the client in a caring and reflective way and building up a relationship of trust. Maturity is an important prerequisite in training as a professional counsellor. To qualify for one of the training courses recognised by the British Association for Counselling, you need to be over 30 and have broad life experience. The majority of counsellors are over 40. Counselling is usually a second career or an avenue for career development, and useful previous career backgrounds include teaching, careers and advisory work, social work, the Church and the health professions.

Most counselling courses are part-time, and include introductory courses run at adult education colleges for people with little or no previous experience in the field. Counsellors work in educational institutions, the workplace, hospitals and medical practices, and for a wide variety of agencies, as well as in private practice. Some specialise in areas such as alcohol, drugs, AIDS, bereavement, cancer, and child abuse.

Some agencies, such as Relate, train their own counsellors. Relate is keen to recruit people from all ethnic groups, and those with disabilities are also welcome to apply. If the work done by Relate interests you, contact the manager of the organisation's centre in your area and ask to have a chat. Should you decide to seek involvement and are accepted for training, this would be spread over 2–2½ years, with certification taking a further six months. The work involves at least three hours counselling a week for 40 weeks a year as well as ongoing study and attendance at training sessions. Rates of pay are set independently at each local centre.

Fostering

Caring for children in your own home while their parents are unable to do so is an important social service provided at a personal level. Some of the children you would be asked to foster might be difficult and disturbed, and many would be confused because of a major disruption in their lives. Their ages can range from infant to teenager, and carers may be asked to foster for anything from a day to several years.

Training is needed and carers receive untaxed allowances to cover their costs. Some agencies also pay carers a separate fee. To find out more, contact the social services department of your local authority.

Charities

If you want to work for a charity, either on a paid or voluntary basis, you have no shortage of choice. There are over 170,000 of them, and new ones are constantly springing up.

Charities require a variety of skills, ranging from fundraising and publicity to accountancy and administration. As one national newspaper put it, 'Charities today mean serious business and seek people with a professional approach to run them.'

Skilled fundraisers are in demand and, according to the Institute of Charity Fundraising Managers, 'Prospects are good both for the mature entrant and those seeking their first career.' There are no formal entry requirements and the main form of training is by short in-service courses.

Voluntary work

There is a constant and increasing demand for volunteers to work for charities and community projects. Opportunities are available to work with children and young people, the elderly, the disabled, the mentally ill, in hospitals and for environmental causes. The work can involve fundraising, counselling, administration, publicity and a variety of other functions. Some organisations offer out-of-pocket expenses, pocket money and, in a few cases, payment for your time.

Your local Citizens' Advice Bureau or public library should be able to provide contacts at the charities seeking volunteers.

RELIGIOUS MINISTRY

More than a job

Most religious denominations welcome applications from mature candidates for ordination, but they are required to have a strong sense of vocation, integrity, intellectual ability, leadership qualities, and the ability to cope with a career that is a way of life rather than a job.

Although some denominations and religious orders have been having difficulty attracting sufficient numbers of suitable applicants for ordination training, selection standards remain high. For many courses, however, entry and training requirements are modified to accommodate well-motivated mature candidates. Courses may be full- or part-time and based on a combination of college attendance and parish work.

In this section the focus is on opportunities for career changers in the larger branches of the Christian Church in the UK. Space limitations preclude coverage of every denomination, or of the other major faiths practised in Britain's multi-ethnic society.

The Anglican Communion

In addition to the Church of England, the Anglican Communion in the UK also includes the Church in Wales, the Scottish Episcopal

Church and the Church of Scotland. Entry requirements and training arrangements vary slightly, but all consider applicants over 40 on their merits.

Church of England

Candidates over 40 for the ordained ministry normally follow either a two year full-time or a three year part-time course. They take the General Ministerial Examination (GME) and subjects are assessed by essays marked externally.

This is how some of the theological training establishments view applicants over 40:

> We are happy to recruit them so long as they demonstrate evidence of being able to cope with the course. We would prefer normal entry qualifications (five O levels and two A levels) but, if these have not been achieved, we look for evidence that the student has the necessary potential, motivation and knowledge. (*Trinity College, Bristol*)

> We will consider for admission anyone recommended by a Bishop's Selection Conference, regardless of age. We do not require any entry qualification, except for a satisfactory interview. (*Lincoln Theological College*)

> It is impossible to generalise on how they perform. Some are 40-plus and wise and mature. For some, 20 year's experience equals one year's experience, repeated 20 times. Some find it hard to be a 'student', some do not. Some feel de-skilled, some are only too glad to have left their previous occupation. (*Ripon College, Cuddesdon, Oxon*)

Neil left a career in agriculture and food processing at the age of 51 to train for the ministry, and found 'surprisingly few difficulties' on the two-year course at the Lincoln Theological College designed to cater for the needs of older students. The course was based on written work without exams, but with external assessment by the Advisory Council for the Church Ministry (ACCM). 'Teaching was carried out in small groups, and seminars and tutorials were more common than lectures,' said Neil. 'My fees were paid from central church funds and my diocese made up the funds necessary to support my wife and youngest daughter, who was 18 when I began.'

In November 1992 the Church of England Synod voted in favour of admitting women to the priesthood. The decision has to be ratified by Parliament, but it is anticipated that ordination of women priests could begin in 1994. The alienation and frustration by women who have previously entered the ministry was highlighted by Marianne, a former teacher who took her theological training in her forties. 'The study and training are fully equal for men and women,' she said. 'At the end men have a wide choice of positions to go to, whereas those for women are limited. At the end of the first year men are ordained to the priesthood, thereby becoming able to practice the full sacramental ministry.' Despite these limitations, Marianne found that her work in the church had offered 'many delightful surprises and much that is worthwhile'.

Other middle-aged entrants to the C of E ministry from whom I heard included a chartered civil engineer, a solicitor, a Royal Air Force technician, a midwifery tutor, an agriculturalist, a housewife and a physicist.

There are also opportunities in the church to become a lay worker and take responsibilities in such areas as administration, teaching, race relations and media work.

Roman Catholic Church

Mature men are encouraged to offer themselves as candidates for the priesthood in the Roman Catholic Church. The normal seminary training course spans at least six years, but older candidates may be allowed to take a special four year course at the Beda College in Rome.

Providing they are fit, of the required IQ and capable of being adaptable, mature candidates may be admitted up to about age 55, said the Director of Vocations for the Roman Catholic Diocese of Leeds. His opposite number in the Westminster Diocese said more older men were coming forward and they often had more of a commitment than younger students.

In exceptional cases the upper age limit can be quite flexible. Peter, a former military intelligence officer and civil servant, became a priest at the age of 67 after entering the religious order, the Institute of Charity. He decided to devote himself to the religious life after his wife died and his children reached maturity. After an 18 month novitiate he took vows (poverty, chastity and obedience) and was placed in charge of the order's library. 'I was blissfully content with a life of prayer, meditation, outdoor manual work and librarianship,' he said, 'and had no thought of priesthood until I was told the order wished me to study for ordination. I felt obliged to do so because of my vow of obedience.'

Following ordination, Peter continued his studies for another year and worked part-time as a priest in the mother-house and on supply. Since then he has been engaged in parish work. 'As a priest in a parish I find that my years and my varied experience in life are an advantage,' he said. 'I find it easy to relate to people of any age.' For those who feel called to the religious life, he advised, 'Have a go. But if you are doubtful, or become doubtful, about your vocation, get out before you are ordained. There is no more miserable creature than an unhappy priest.'

Religious orders

There are religious communities for men and women in both the Anglican and Roman Catholic churches. The orders may dedicate themselves to teaching, social work, nursing or contemplation, and some are changing with the times, widening their activities and modifying or abandoning their traditional attire. Entry and training requirements vary, and some courses may involve simultaneous study for a university degree.

In the past many older women with a vocation for the convent life have been unable to fulfil it because age prevented their acceptance by one of the religious orders. An opportunity for such women was created with the establishment, near Rugby in 1983, of the Congregation of Mary Mother of the Church, an order especially for mature women up to the age of 65. The order has flourished and opened further houses. New entrants, who are generally between their late thirties and mid-sixties, undergo a three-month postulancy and then return home for a month to give both them and the congregation a chance to evaluate their suitability to become a novice. A one-year novitiate follows and then three years temporary profession, at the end of which entrants decide whether to make a life commitment or return to secular life.

Sister Patricia, the widow of a doctor and mother of five grown-up children, said she entered the convent in her late fifties because 'I felt the need to wait on the Lord for the remaining years of my life.' After entry she found the mental and physical aspects of the life 'far more strenuous than I had envisaged, but the prayer life, silence and meditation were quite wonderful.' Apart from the 'big challenge' of community living, the problems were the lack of freedom to travel or sometimes to relax when it is not feasible. 'Good health is a basic priority,' she said, 'and cheerfulness and willingness to "give" and to make allowances are also a great bonus. Punctuality and fidelity to the prayer life in a truly spiritual sense are vital.'

Methodists

Before applying to become a candidate for the Methodist ministry, applicants must prepare by becoming a local preacher and pass examinations in Christian doctrine and biblical knowledge. Most then go on to a full-time course at a theological college, although it is possible to train on a part-time basis.

United Reformed Church

Candidates for the URC ministry must be recommended by their local church, District Council and Provincial Ministerial Committee in their area. They then follow a three or four year course at a theological college. Part-time training is available to qualify as a member of the Church's unpaid auxiliary ministry.

The URC's secretary for ministerial training told me, 'People making a radical change in their lives and starting a second or third career is a significant factor in ministerial recruitment to the United Reformed Church.' He said entry qualifications for the Church's various training programmes were 'realistic in terms of past experience and future study.'

Janet, the wife of a URC minister, began her ministerial training at Mansfield College, Oxford, at the age of 50. She enjoyed the course, but said the main difficulty was that it was residential. 'Luckily I was able to return home at weekends to my other life (husband, family, etc.),' she added, 'but this did mean that I had to complete all my academic studies within a four-day period each week.' She felt that anyone, whatever their age, who believes they have a call to the Christian ministry, should 'just go ahead and see what happens.' The preliminaries to acceptance for training can sometimes take well over a year and 'will certainly test the call — and you.'

Baptists

Candidates for the accredited ministry of the Baptist Church are normally accepted up to the age of 55, but must be recommended by their local church, then assessed by the Baptist association to which it belongs, before being interviewed by a theological college. The course lasts from three to six years depending on the candidate's qualifications and background. Mature candidates may fulfil the training requirements for ordination by full-time or by church-based part-time study.

'We have a small but significant number of people over 40 coming forward for the Baptist Ministry,' said the Director of Admissions at the Baptists' Spurgeon's College in London. 'The entry requirements for them are the same as for others, laying stress on call and gifting rather than academic ability. We do make certain allowances for their age in terms of course and flexible training methods.'

As a factory production manager, Brian's responsibilities included stock control. He took stock of his own life in his early 40s and decided that his future lay in the Church. 'I had no great desire to take the next natural step to promotion,' he said, 'and other people were encouraging me towards the ministry.' At the age of 44 he began a four year training course at the Northern Baptist College, Manchester, and graduated with a degree in theology awarded by Manchester University. After ordination he became Baptist minister in an Anglican/Baptist local ecumenical project in London. He found his previous industrial experience a great asset in relating to people. 'Do not get carried away by the idea of "call", he said. 'Seek advice from as many people as possible. Only enter training when you can truthfully say, "I can do no other".'

Unitarian Church

The upper age for entry to training for the Unitarian ministry is 55. Depending on previous qualifications, candidates take a degree or diploma course lasting from two to four years. Entrants must have the support of their local congregation, a sense of vocation and its implications, a good general education, academic potential, and stability in relationships.

Charles, a former cabaret artist, who was motivated by an 'inner compulsion to address the imbalance between spiritual and materialist values', trained at the Manchester Unitarian College in his early forties. He helped finance his course by performing in clubs at weekends, and also ministered to two churches, completing a three year course in two. He found the experience 'hard but exhilarating.'

Congregationalists

Part-time training courses are organised by the Congregational Federation for people aged 18 to 70 who wish to serve in the organisation's churches as lay preachers, pastors and ministers. There are no tuition fees.

Salvation Army

Members of the Salvation Army up to the age of 40 may, if they have the backing of their corps, take a two year training course to become officers. In the selection process spiritual qualities are rated more important than academic qualifications, but adequate standards are required in English and mathematics.

The Salvation Army also employs lay people, professionally qualified staff and volunteers in its various social service undertakings.

CHECK LIST

- Before considering religious ministry be certain of your vocation.

- Be prepared to meet exacting selection standards.

- Realise that you will be taking on a way of life, not just a job.

7

The Protectors

THE LEGAL PROFESSION

The system
In England and Wales the legal profession has two main branches
— barristers and solicitors — though their future roles have been
under scrutiny and the subject of reform proposals. A similar
system operates in Northern Ireland, but the Scottish legal system
is distinctly different, though also having two branches, solicitors
and advocates.

There is no age bar for entry, and the problem for latecomers to
law is not so much the academic training involved, though this is
exacting, but finding a firm to take them on as a pupil, particularly
in the case of barristers. Apart from private practice, employment
opportunities for lawyers also exist in industry, the Civil Service
and local government.

Barrister
In their traditional role barristers pass down their advice through
solicitors and conduct cases in court, enjoying a virtual monopoly in
the representation of clients in the High Court. Income is likely to
be low at first, but success brings high rewards. This profession is a
daunting option for the latecomer, however, given the difficulty of
obtaining a pupillage and the length of time it takes to build up a
professional reputation sufficient to earn a good living.

Solicitor
Solicitors handle most ordinary legal business for their clients. It is
usual to take a degree followed by professional examinations and
two years as an articled clerk before qualification. In addition to
appearing in court and briefing barristers, the work of solicitors
includes handling the legal aspects of property sales, wills, divorces
and taxation matters.

For Wendy, a former secretary who qualified as a solicitor in her early forties, the route to professional success was not an easy one. First she obtained two A levels (law at evening class and sociology by correspondence), then earned an external law degree at the University of North London, and finally, after three attempts, passed the solicitors' professional examination. After qualifying, she became a partner in a London suburban practice, mainly handling conveyancing, probate, wills and matrimonial work. 'There is very high job satisfaction, helping people and getting results,' she said. 'I enjoy being well-known in the district and, with a good income, I have no more money problems. I enjoy the personal autonomy, the intellectual stimulation and the feeling of self-worth which was lacking in my previous career. I work very long hours. To some extent this is my personal choice, but it does mean that I don't have time for all the other things I want to do.'

Sally, a former hospital chaplain, began training as a solicitor at 46 because she felt the need to work in an area that offered help to people but challenged her in an intellectual rather than an emotional direction. She undertook the Law Society of Scotland's pre-diploma traineeship programme, which enabled her to study for a professional legal qualification while working full-time during the day for an Edinburgh law firm. 'Much of the study has had to be done independently,' she said. 'The disparity between theory and practice can seem disproportionately wide and confusing when one is first starting, especially in a very pragmatic discipline such as law. Trainees are obviously paid the very minimum since that is their worth to the firm. All the solicitors in my firm are younger than I am, but I don't personally find it difficult doing things for them, asking questions, and generally taking directions, because this is a learning/training experience.'

Legal executive
Legal executives assist solicitors in a range of professional duties, and often specialise in particular types of business, such as property conveyancing, litigation and wills. A significant number of men and women who qualify are over 40, but the Institute of Legal Executives advised that it is quite difficult for mature entrants with no experience of legal work to find a training vacancy, particularly if they need to earn a salary.

Most mature students taking part in the Institute's training scheme have worked in clerical or secretarial capacities in legal offices, and use the scheme and the qualification as a means of advancement.

There is no Scottish equivalent to this profession.

Licensed conveyancer

Licensed conveyancing is a relatively new profession, created under legislation passed in 1985. Its practitioners handle the transfer of property rights from one person to another. To qualify you are required to pass an examination set by the Council of Licensed Conveyancers and have two years practical training with an established licensed conveyancer or solicitor.

SECURITY AND PROTECTION SERVICES

The police

If you can meet the fitness, character and citizenship requirements there is still a chance of starting a police career when you are nearing or even past 40, especially if you have recently served in the armed forces or the merchant navy. Chief constables are able to exercise discretion when it comes to the age of recruits to their forces. The Home Office stresses that 'There is no upper age limit (within reason!) except for the graduate accelerated promotion scheme, for which you must be under 30.' There are no minimum height requirements as there used to be, but you must be in good health, have a good physique and high standard of eyesight.

An opportunity for part-time police work is offered by the special constabulary. The upper age limit for entry is 50, and the job includes a free uniform and expenses.

Other possibilities which might be worth exploring are specialist forces, such as the Ministry of Defence Police and British Transport Police.

Traffic warden

If you enjoy working outside, are under 60, and possess such qualities as politeness, firmness and tact, you could qualify as a traffic warden. Good health and eyesight are important. You may not win many friends, but you might be able to influence people, at least with regard to their parking habits!

Security work

Recruits to the industrial and commercial security industry are mainly adults, and a sizeable proportion are over 40. To join them you will need to be fit and have good character references. Experience in the police or the armed forces is a strong recommendation, and some well–qualified entrants from those backgrounds are sometimes able to move into management positions in the industry.

Opportunities for middle-agers to work as security guards exist either in-house or with a security organisation which hires out guards under contract. The work ranges from guarding business or industrial premises to accompanying goods and cash in transit.

A range of training courses, including correspondence tuition, is provided by the International Institute of Security in conjunction with the City and Guilds of London Institute.

Private investigator

This is frequently a second career, and there are no age or legal barriers to entry. The profession is open equally to men and women, but it is valuable, if not essential, to have had some relevant experience in the police, armed forces or the legal profession. Even with this kind of background, it is worth trying to get some 'sharp end' experience with an existing investigation agency before branching out on your own.

The work can range from tracing debtors and other missing persons to matrimonial enquiries and investigating industrial espionage. There is a good deal of routine work and much time spent sifting and checking information and making telephone calls. The hours are sometimes long and tedious, but the pay can be good and there may be opportunities for travel, and occasionally some exciting moments.

As former policeman turned private detective, James Ackroyd, points out in his useful book *The Investigator*, 'this job is not suitable for the squeamish, unworldly individual' but it is a 'useful, honourable, and also a very necessary and indispensable social service to the community.'

Parkkeeper

If you fancy a stroll in the park as part of your daily routine, this might be an option to consider. There is no formal upper age limit for entry, but you must be fit. Experience in the armed services or security work is likely to enhance your prospects of appointment.

Trading standards officer

Local authority based trading standards officers are responsible for enforcing consumer protection legislation, and maintaining a fair system of trading between traders and between them and their customers.

No upper age limit is specified for entry, but relevant experience in such areas as laboratory testing, health and hygiene and customer relations is helpful. Business experience or work with the police or other law enforcement agencies is also valuable. You need to be fairly robust as occasional heavy work can be involved.

Training is on the job, and a diploma course can be taken by day release.

Environmental health officer

Formerly called public health inspectors, these officials are concerned with enforcement of regulations designed to protect and promote a healthy living and working environment. They spend much of their time inspecting restaurants, workplaces and other premises to check that health, hygiene and safety requirements are being met.

There is no formal upper age restriction on entry, but officers are normally required to have a degree or diploma in environmental health.

Immigration officer

These officers are civil servants who work under the jurisdiction of the Home Office. They are based primarily at airports and seaports and their basic role is the prevention of illegal immigration. It can be a tough, demanding job requiring considerable tact and firmness. Training is largely on the job, and the normal upper age limit for entry is 50.

Customs and excise officer

Although customs and excise officers are perhaps most familiar through their work at airports and seaports checking travellers' baggage for illegal imports, they also carry various other important roles concerned with such matters as VAT and collection of duties on petrol, tobacco and alcoholic beverages.

The Customs and Excise Service will consider candidates up to the age of 50.

Coastguard

HM Coastguard, which is under the jurisdiction of the Department of Transport, may take entrants up to 49, providing that they have previous sea-going experience or are qualified in search and rescue work.

Prison Service

To be considered for recruitment as a prison officer you must be under 50 (in Scotland no more than 42, or 47 for ex-armed forces personnel), but you don't need any formal qualifications. However, the Service looks for patience, understanding, leadership and common sense. The selectors will be even happier if you can offer some trade or professional expertise which you may be able to pass on to inmates.

Apart from opportunities to serve as an instructor, you can also specialise as a dog handler, security or hospital officer. There are height, nationality and fitness requirements, and you have to take an aptitude test. The sectors require references and will, naturally, look very carefully at any convictions.

Upper age limits for recruitment to the prison governor class (normally at assistant governor level) are the same as for prison officers.

MILITARY SERVICE

Armed forces

Reductions in manning levels have diminished opportunities for mature entry to the armed forces, but a few doors remain slightly ajar, if not wide open.

The Royal Navy will consider medical practitioners up to the age of 44 and the Royal Army Veterinary Corps has an upper age limit of 41 for recruiting qualified veterinary graduates.

Recruits in ground trades and officer candidates in some non-flying branches up to the age of 39 can be accepted in the Royal Air Force, but the shrinkage in the service means that in practice virtually all manning needs are filled by younger applicants.

Territorial Army (TA)

Forty is the normal upper age limit for entry to the Territorial Army, which offers opportunities in such fields as engineering, transport, medical and signals. Rates of pay are almost on a par with the regular army, and personnel are reimbursed for each day they put in up to 100 days a year. There is also a tax-free annual bounty.

8

The Living World

RURAL PURSUITS

Working out-of-doors in tranquil, often beautiful surroundings, far from the noise, pollution and stresses of urban existence, living close to nature, being your own boss, enjoying the gentle pleasures of rural social life... what more could a jaded townie ask?

What indeed! But before you start packing your bags, ponder the words of some of those who have gone ahead of you. The problems as well as the satisfactions of making a living from the land are reflected in their comments and advice in this chapter.

Should running a three or four hundred-acre spread seem a little too daunting, there are such alternatives as a smallholding, nursery or professional gardening. You could also work for someone else in an agricultural or horticultural enterprise if you have a background in, say, management, mechanics or secretarial work. For such rural occupations as gamekeeper or countryside ranger you would need to have relevant previous experience as well as being physically fit.

Farming
The choices
Farmland covers about four-fifths of the United Kingdom. If you want to run a piece of it, there are three basic choices — livestock, crops, or a mixture of both. While most stay with the more familiar livestock, a few opt for deer, goats, rabbits, llamas, snails, and even fish. The choice will be partly dictated by the geographical location of the farm.

Preparing yourself
The vital first step is to do your homework as thoroughly as possible. Tune in to farming programmes on radio and television, read farming magazines like *Farmers Weekly* or *Farming News* (you should find copies in your local public library), visit agricultural shows, even take farm holidays. Seek advice from organisations such as the Careers

Education and Training Information Centre of the Royal Agricultural Society and the Agricultural Training Board.

If possible try to spend some time working on the kind of enterprise you would like to run, whether it's an arable farm in lush green, rolling acres, a remote hill farm, or a piggery. Work unpaid if necessary, pick the brains of the old hands and don't be afraid to collect a few callouses in exchange for some invaluable practical experience.

Many newcomers do most of their learning on the job, but a number of contributors stressed the value of a basic level course at an agricultural college or a college of further education, if time and circumstances allow. A wide variety of courses suitable for the beginner are available, both part- and full-time; some require no academic qualifications for entry. Many vocationally-oriented courses are available through the National Examining Board for Agriculture and Horticulture and Allied Industries (NEBAHAI).

Finding a farm

Once you have made up your mind to take the plunge, the first task is to find a farm that you can afford and will be able to run. This may take some time, as Chris and Janet, a Gloucestershire couple, discovered. They spent 2½ years searching before they found the place they wanted — a 70-acre dairy holding in Dyfed. Both 'townies' by birth, Chris had worked previously for other farmers in various capacities and Janet was employed in local government.

They felt it was imperative to employ a land agent to guide their choice. 'He's the one who knows about possible sales, the correct prices and, of course, he will visit the farm and assess its viability for you,' said Janet. 'We consider the £1,600 we paid for ours as money well spent. He prevented some blunders on our part on points we had never considered. He always did an "instant" feasibility study on each farm we looked at so we knew what the possible income could be on that holding. He's your most valuable assistant; don't contemplate a move without him.'

Business acumen needed

Good organisation and sound financial management are vital to running a modern, efficient farm. Even well-run holdings can sometimes struggle to be profitable, particularly in the early stages. These comments reflect the experiences of a cross-section of contributors:

Anyone contemplating farming today should approach it in a

totally hard-headed manner. They should be computer literate and try to be as little persuaded as possible by the more romantic notions of country life. The adage that 'a fool and his money are soon parted' applies to anyone approaching agriculture. *(former owner of plant hire company; fruit farm, Kent)*

Change your accountant *tout de suite* if he doesn't do your books within three months of the financial year end. The best tax and VAT advice you can get is from the Inland Revenue and Customs and Excise — and it's free. *(former management consultant; 106 acres, Perthshire)*.

Consult the Agricultural Development and Advisory Service (ADAS) or an agricultural college in the area for information on local conditions. Spend about half of your capital on the farm purchase, which will allow sufficient capital to be retained as buffer for the first year. Do not rush into altering/modernising, but go through at least one complete year to learn needs and new environment. *(former shipping company executive; 141 acres, Aberdeenshire)*

Building up the farm
Many newcomers find much work is needed to get their farm into shape for efficient operation. Here is a sample of what some of them had to cope with:

One of the biggest headaches was the lack of adequate fencing, which gave rise to a monumental amount of work and a lot of exercise in retrieving wandering animals. I had to carry out extensive restorations to the farmhouse, fence the whole farm and generally improve the land and facilities *(retired medical scientist; 64 acres, Dyfed)*

The land had been somewhat neglected in the previous five years, and was generally overrun with all the well-known weeds. My first job was to build a sheep shed. Then we started on the bracken, docks and thistles. After stocking with sheep, we had to replace the hay barn. When that was finished weeds still loomed large in my life. I had 80 tonnes of lime spread on the more accessible parts of the fields and I spread a further 15 tonnes by hand on the steeper slopes. *(ex-army officer; 80 acres, Argyllshire)*

A neglected property takes a lot of work and patience to bring into line. Above all you need resources to withstand four or five years to get into profit. *(former newsagent; 47 acres, Larne, Northern Ireland)*

Neighbours

There are some basic approaches worth adopting if you want to establish and maintain a happy relationship with your farming neighbours. This contribution from Reginald, who gave up medical practice in Birmingham to farm 160 acres in Devon, reflects the kind of advice received from contributors in various parts of the UK:

> Don't evangelise. Ask for advice from local farmers; this is a great oiler of wheels. Be prepared for the fact that they will all be watching for you to fall flat on our face. Shut up initially about hunting. It is essential to keep your perimeter fences stockproof. The man who told me he had never seen a worse piece of ploughing in his life (my first attempt) offered to lend me £4000 worth of equipment to stop my hay heating up because I had cut it too early. Never decide that you will show the locals how to do anything — until asked, and you will be in time. The Womens' Institute is very valuable if the wives can be interested. They meet people, learn the best butcher, baker, etc., and can also fit into the rota for picking up newspapers and other things, which are not delivered. The old days of fishmongers, butchers, bakers and tinkers calling every week are gone. Market day is important both to see and be seen.

The problems

The difficulty many farmers have found in making a decent living has driven a growing number off the land in recent years. In addition to bureaucracy and the vagaries of the market and the British climate, these were some of the down-to-earth realities of farming life noted by respondents:

> Be prepared to live in trousers, sweaters and wellies. Remember, farming is all about muck — it's everywhere! *(former nurse; 36 acres, Peebleshire)*

> On my type of farm you must be prepared to work seven days a week, 365 days a year and forfeit annual holidays. *(former works director; 445 acres, North Yorkshire)*

> Several suppliers have tried to pull tricks on us, and two have been reported to trading standards officers; another we refused to pay because of a fraudulent invoice. The general standard of

suppliers to the farming industry falls well below that in other industries. Most farmers don't know how to challenge big companies who try to rip them off. (*ex-managing director, chemical industry; 150 acres, Lancashire*)

When we moved north to Scotland the problems of gaining credibility began. We met resistance from a few locals who made it quite clear that they resented the affluent southerners buying their farms, but contractors and suppliers' representatives seemed to appreciate the influx of new money. The seasons up here are 4-6 weeks later than Central/South England. (*former company executive; Aberdeenshire*)

We've made hundreds of mistakes, but I expect we'll make loads more, like buying a ram, not checking him, and then wondering why we had no lambs. It wasn't until we sheared him that we found his bits had gone; he'd been castrated, so he went in the freezer. We weren't at all sure about eating him, but he tasted good. (*former housewife; four acres, North Yorkshire*)

The rewards

For most latecomers to farming the rewards go beyond mere financial returns, which in any case may often be modest, and occasionally non-existent. This is what some had to say:

In farming I have found a worthwhile meaning to life instead of front-line hassle, and my family and I have control of our destiny in one of the most beautiful parts of the British Isles. It is the best decision of my lifetime. (*former marketing executive; 98 acres, Dyfed*)

There is more in life than money. I liked my job but hated commuting. My interests lay in the country. The rewards include the pleasure of seeing sunrise and sunset, the birds and beasts, wild and domestic, and the satisfaction, even at great cost, of being your own boss. (*ex-London stockbroker; 487 acres, Aberdeenshire*)

Farming offers a very healthy way of life at a time when one might be tempted to sit about too much. In the first three months I lost three stone in weight, and was immensely pleased. (*former teacher; 100 acres, Devon*)

Starting a farming venture where children can participate has a very beneficial effect on family life as the kids 'muck in', add their interest and energies, and don't get fussed at home. By contrast, venturing into farming when the children were younger would have brought problems and split loyalties. (*former overseas development worker; 11 acres, Berkshire*)

The highlight of my career was this very morning seeing the first litter born (15 alive). It's the start of a whole new life for me. (*pig breeder; 70 acres, Suffolk*)

We don't make any money out of it as we really are quite remote, but we are enjoying ourselves. (*ex-nurse; crofter, Ross-shire*)

We left behind security, a mortgage, prestige and a lot of friends, but have gained peace of mind, a love of animals and their companionship, and a feeling of achievement by sheer hard work. Life for us certainly began at 40-plus. (*former psychiatric social worker; 40 acres, Dyfed*)

Check list:
- Expect long hours and hard, physical work.
- Budget carefully and allow for sufficient capital to tide you over the first year.
- Cultivate your neighbours and get involved in the life of the community.

Horticulture
A major industry
The dividing line between agriculture and horticulture is not clear-cut, and much of what was said in the preceding paragraphs is equally relevant to horticultural enterprises.

Horticulture is a major industry whose activities range from the commercial production of vegetables, fruit and flowers to the establishment and maintenance of parks, sports grounds and private estates, as well as supporting and servicing gardening. Each year the industry attracts many mature entrants, some of whom acquired their taste for the work through tending their own gardens. Many ease their way into the business by spending a period with a nursery, garden centre, landscape contractor, or local authority, looking after parks and public open spaces.

To find out more about what you and the industry might have to offer each other, contact the Institute of Horticulture. If you tell them which part of the industry interests you, they can put you in touch with an appropriate member of their careers panel.

A variety of full-time, part-time or correspondence courses is available from BTEC to degree level, and among the establishments offering training are the Royal Horticultural Society and the Royal Botanical Gardens in Kew and Edinburgh.

Nurseries and garden centres
One of the popular options with late starters in commercial horticulture is the running of a nursery or garden centre.

A nursery was the choice of Janet, formerly a theatre nurse at a children's hospital. She took a two-year course in nursery practice at a horticultural college, gaining a distinction, before setting up her business in Worcestershire. She specialises in hardy geraniums and less common herbaceous plants and shrubs, and has created considerable interest among plant collectors. Among the problems Janet has encountered have been persuading suppliers to deliver relatively small quantities and finding competent, qualified relief staff. 'Make sure your family are as happy about your commitment as you are,' she advised. 'To be open six days a week from Easter to late October and every weekend is extremely restricting for everybody. It is a stimulating and satisfying experience but you need to achieve continual growth to maintain the interest, which of course increases the workload.'

The stress associated with his previous career prompted Ron, former director of a shipping line, to switch to a career as a nurseryman, which he believed would offer a better quality of life for his family. He found that being the 'owner-driver' of the business enabled him to make and implement plans quickly, and though more strenuous, his new occupation provided a better balance between mental and physical work. He recommended a thorough physical check-up before taking up this kind of work.

Made redundant by a horticultural manufacturing firm in his late forties, and with a family of five 'totally without any means of support', John eventually came up with a novel answer to the headache of finding a new living. He dug up the carefully nurtured lawns in his quarter-acre garden in Essex and planted the herb feverfew, which is taken by sufferers from migraine, arthritis and a variety of other disorders and stress-related problems. After harvesting the crop he and his wife clean it by hand, taking care to remove anything that is not pure feverfew. Then they dry it, using a professional drying tunnel — in the early days they did this in their lounge – and cure it before packaging by hand, with John funnelling and his wife sealing. The packets are posted to a growing band of clients in Britain and abroad, and an impressive file of letters testifies to the beneficial effects of the product.

Gardening

There are probably few more popular pastimes among the over-40s than gardening, and one who turned her hobby into a profession was Gina, a former Middlesex school teacher. Her first move was to take a Royal Horticultural Society course, studying one evening a week for two years at a horticultural college. She found the course 'a wonderful background', and, after becoming a full-time professional maintenance gardener, was 'flooded with work'.

Gina said there is a dearth of gardeners with real plant knowledge to support elderly gardeners or those with large areas to maintain. 'I found people's attitude to a lady gardener slightly suspicious,' she told me. "How can you do the digging? How can you cope with that tree?" etc. But once you prove yourself there is no trouble; in fact, a real respect grows between employer and employee. I make a living wage but had to draw in the reins because of the large reduction in salary compared to my teaching days. However, the tremendous joy and satisfaction the job gives me far exceeds the need to earn more. It has opened up a whole new world.'

Wine production

There are over 400 vineyards in England, Wales and the Channel Islands, many of them run by people who entered the business after

40, and interest in wine production is growing, according to the English Vineyards Association (EVA).

To successfully establish and run a vineyard, however, you need not only considerable capital but patience. It usually takes four years from planting for vines to become productive, and a considerable investment of time and resources is required in ground preparation, fencing and windbreaks, a training system of posts and wires, fertiliser and spraying, pruning and harvesting.

Few vineyard owners in this country depend solely on wine for their livelihood. Some are farmers who have simply diversified, and most vineyards are supplemented by some other activity. Many growers welcome visitors and offer wine tastings.

Roger, a former civil engineer who has established a three-acre vineyard in Oxfordshire, combines wine making with growing asparagus and soft fruit, and makes nearly all his sales from the door. He told me, 'Vineyards are highly capitalised because of the amount of equipment required, especially if a winery is involved. Dependence on second-hand equipment is not satisfactory. A vineyard small enough to be run by a couple without full-time help is too small to be viable. Payment of full-time wages requires a much larger operation, with a consequent move into the wholesale market where competition is fiercer and margins lower.'

Ian attended several seminars and a course on basic viticulture before planting his vineyard in Devon. 'This is not a career for the faint-hearted,' he warned, 'or for those who believe there is money to be made in this country out of growing vines. It is a way of life and many people drop out after a few years because they can't make ends meet. We personally have developed another business using wine as a byproduct, which makes the operation viable.'

If you want to explore the wine business further, imbibe the literature and visit as many vineyards as you can. The EVA will send you a list of them if you enclose a stamped addressed envelope.

Forestry

This is not the easiest of professions to break into after 40, especially if you are looking for an opening with Britain's biggest employer of foresters, the Forestry Commission, or one of the other major organisations in the field. Competition for openings is keen.

The Commission's usual upper age limit for recruits is 40, but it will sometimes consider older candidates with special knowledge and experience. Check with the Forestry Training Council.

Alternatively, if you have sufficient knowledge and some capital you could consider the possibility of becoming a freelance grower. One option that has attracted a number of older people is growing Christmas trees. The secretary of the British Christmas Tree Growers Association warned, however, of the financial risks. 'It is about five years before you see any return on your money,' he said.

For those with an interest in planting, care and conservation of amenity trees and woods, membership of the Arboriculture Association is well worth considering.

Conservation

In addition to forestry and arboriculture, a variety of possibilities is open to those keen to work in occupations which play a part in protecting and nurturing the flora and fauna of the countryside. They include estate management, gamekeeping, and employment as a countryside ranger or warden.

After leaving the Royal Air Force at 40, Richard took City and Guilds day release courses in amenity horticulture and horticulture management, and a variety of short courses in such areas as tractor maintenance, hedge laying, pesticides, youth training and adult teaching. He was able to find employment with a county council as a youth training scheme instructor in conservation and estate management. His responsibilities include a small nursery growing trees and plants and the recovery of plants from areas scheduled for development so that they can be re-introduced after completion of the project. 'My contribution to countryside conservation is very satisfying,' he said, 'and at the same time provides training for youngsters in such areas as forestry contracting, landscaping, nurseries and woodland estates.' Richard also does voluntary work with conservation groups.

CAREERS WITH ANIMALS

Labour of love

For those who enjoy working with animals there is a variety of employment possibilities, but in many cases it has to be largely a labour of love because the work is likely to be low paid. The options include dog training, assisting at boarding kennels and grooming parlours, and working for organisations concerned with the welfare and treatment of animals.

Guide dog training

Some of the most rewarding work in animal training is that carried out at the establishments of the Guide Dogs for the Blind Association. There is no upper age limit for recruitment, and the Association welcomes applications from mature candidates, especially if they have relevant experience. However, competition for places is keen.

Recruits need to be robust and healthy because the work involves walking dogs many miles every day in all weathers. It is also necessary to be literate, numerate, articulate and confident in order to be able to handle all aspects of the job effectively.

Those who display the required practical ability may go on to qualify as guide dog mobility instructors, whose work includes advanced dog training and helping blind people to use their dogs.

Riding instructor

If horses are your particular interest, and you have appropriate experience, you could try qualifying as a riding instructor. Most instructors obtain their credentials from the British Horse Society. There is no age bar, but you need to be fit.

Farrier

Farriery and blacksmithing also provide the opportunity to work with horses, but it is hard physical work and the training course is lengthy and demanding. A farrier has to be capable of shoeing the feet of horses and similar animals to suit all types of work and working conditions.

There is no upper age limit for entry to training, but an apprenticeship of four years, including a probationary period, has to be served. The training must be undertaken with a farrier approved by the Farriers Registration Council, and the cost of the course for entrants in the winter of 1992 was £6000.

Animal welfare worker

Animal welfare agencies, such as the RSPCA and the People's Dispensary for Sick Animals (PDSA), offer various career possibilities.

The normal upper age limit for trainee inspectors with the RSPCA is 40 (42 for personnel leaving the armed forces), and, though experience of working with animals is not considered essential, the Society prefers candidates who have a background of working with the public. There is keen competition for entry to the seven-month training course, and recruits must have a good general education, a driving licence, and be able to swim 50 metres fully clothed. In Scotland the SSPCA will consider well qualified candidates up to 50, and they like them to have experience of working with animals, preferably farm animals. The training normally lasts six months.

The PDSA said that opportunities for the over-40s tended to be mainly in such areas as administration, fund-raising and regional shop organising.

Veterinary nurse

While middle-agers have little realistic hope of being accepted for training as veterinary surgeons, there are opportunities for a rewarding career in veterinary nursing.

The practical nursing course can be completed on a full- or part-time basis, and the theory may be studied by correspondence. To enrol on the course, for which the Royal College of Veterinary Surgeons sets the examinations, you need to be employed in an approved veterinary practice.

Elizabeth, formerly a teacher of the deaf, said she had never regretted her change of career to veterinary nursing, although it had meant a considerably reduced income. Employed in a small practice for five years, she told me, 'I find I have a lot of responsibility and can use my initiative more than if I was part of a larger nursing team. I particularly enjoy talking to clients and being able to offer them advice on general pet health care and related matters. I have found it a very satisfying career and would recommend it to anyone, providing they are not contemplating it as a sole source of income. I am fortunate that we can live quite comfortably on my husband's income and use mine for "extras".'

It is possible to work in a veterinary practice without taking the nursing qualifications, and some vets prefer to train their own nurses.

Dog warden

Self-employed central heating engineer and dog lover Brian Wilson made a radical career change when, at the age of 42, he became the dog warden for Bournemouth. 'I was selected from 20 applicants, and at the time was one of only four wardens in the country,' he said, 'but it cost me a big drop in income.'

The job involves containing and removing stray dogs, warning and prosecuting owners for infringements of by-laws concerning control of dogs, investigating complaints of noisy dogs, and responding to complaints about the breeding and keeping of dogs. The service is radio controlled and the work programme computerised.

'The town is now virtually free of stray dogs,' Brian told me. His main problems are with owners who do not wish to learn and never heed good advice regarding the handling and control of their animals.

In his spare time Brian teaches courses in dog handling and obedience training and competes and judges at shows.

Self-employment

Most people who start businesses concerned with animals have first acquired experience of handling them through a hobby or leisure interest. Among the more popular choices are running boarding kennels, catteries and grooming parlours and caring for sick animals. Breeding, training and showing dogs and cats are also popular, as is the breeding of cage birds and fish, but these activities are generally pursued as hobbies rather than as a primary source of income.

Breeding/showing

To breed or board dogs and cats you need a licence from your local authority. It is also a good idea to join the association for the particular breed in which you specialise, and to attend shows as often as possible and learn from successful breeders. Dog breeders should also get advice from the Kennel Club.

While breeding can be profitable with breeds that have larger litters, it can be a round-the-clock, seven days-a-week occupation, with feed and veterinary expenses absorbing a sizeable chunk of your income.

After a quarter of a century in the film business, Ann, a former casting director, turned her talents to showing dogs. She produced a show champion, won a number of other top prizes, and then decided to concentrate on breeding deerhounds. 'Dogs totally altered my life,' she said. 'I switched from Chanel suits to wellie boots, from thespians to deerhounders — the name for deerhound people — and after 42 years of smoking I gave it up and took to walking for two hours a day.'

Elsie, a pensioner who had been showing her miniature long-haired dachshunds seriously for only three years, and won over 300 prizes, told me, 'I am hoping to learn to steward and perhaps in a few years to judge too. I aim to breed the best I can, with super temperaments, and hopefully continue showing, though it is getting rather expensive to show nowadays.'

Training

David, a former toolmaker, who spent 22 years as a trainer and instructor with the Guide Dogs for the Blind Association, later moved on to establish his own dog training and behavioural advice service. To help him in his new career, he took training courses in personal selling skills, practical marketing, advertising and promotion, and customer care. His work ranges from basic dog training to advising on behaviour problems. To others aspiring to this sort of work his advice is: 'Keep things simple, make sure you know your subject, and have "stickability". The owners trust you to help them; make sure you give them only the best at all times.'

Courses

Courses are available at further education and agricultural colleges, and at the Animal Care College and the College of Animal Welfare in such skills as running kennels, training, breeding, showing, judging and animal care.

Think twice!

For anyone seriously considering a career involving animals, the Universities Federation for Animal Welfare (UFAW) advised: 'Think twice before deciding to work with animals. It may not be quite as you imagine. Your love of animals must be realistic, not sentimental. The work is often dirty and smelly, and you may have to deal with and even humanely kill sick or severely injured animals.'

The UFAW will send you a useful free leaflet about careers with animals (remember to enclose a stamped addressed envelope).

BUSINESS A BIT SLOW?

9

Working for Leisure

THE LEISURE INDUSTRY

This industry embraces a wide and varied range of entertainment, cultural activities, travel and sport. Mature entrants are drawn from many different backgrounds, such as management, retailing, teaching, theatre, and the armed forces. A number have done voluntary work in areas like children's play or nature conservation, or with sporting or cultural enterprises.

ARTS ADMINISTRATION

This is a specialised field within the leisure industry, involving such responsibilities as planning exhibitions and concerts, managing orchestras and theatre administration. The number of openings is limited, and administrative or secretarial experience, and some links with the visual or performing arts are significant advantages.

TRAVEL AND TOURISM

Individual travel agencies and tour operators set their own age limits for recruitment, but a pleasant, helpful personality and a background in a field such as retailing or office administration will help offset any reservations on the part of potential employers about taking on older staff. Keyboard skills may also enhance your prospects.

Apart from counter jobs in travel agencies, a variety of career possibilities exist for mature entrants, including such work as couriers, resort representatives, 'meeters and greeters' at airports, guides taking groups on walking tours of city sights, and lecturers at historical centres of interest. For appointments as couriers, guides and overseas representatives one or more languages is helpful, as is experience of nursing, teaching or other jobs involved in helping people.

A wide range of training courses is available and can be taken part-time, full-time or by correspondence. Standard entry requirements may be waived for mature students. The National Training

Board of the Association of British Travel Agents (ABTA) prides itself that its courses make provision for anyone 'irrespective of their colour, age, sex, their employment status or their current level of qualifications.' Courses for tourist guides generally last at least six months, and some are offered under the auspices of regional tourist boards. After qualifying through examinations, both written and practical, guides are awarded a 'blue badge' and may be eligible for membership of the Guild of Guide Lecturers.

While previous employment in the travel industry is the most usual background of late starters who set up their own agencies, not all have this experience. Some coming from such fields as general management, finance or secretarial work have built up extremely successful travel agencies.

Apart from expenditure on premises, fittings and equipment, outgoings may include the cost of joining ABTA and the International Air Transport Association (IATA). ABTA membership imposes certain requirements with regard to staffing and financial resources, including the lodging of a bond to help safeguard customers of a member firm in the event of it going bankrupt. IATA membership is essential if you want to issue airline tickets rather than simply book them.

Several contributors warned against expecting to make large profits from a travel agency. Here is a representative selection of their comments and advice:

> Know your product. Make sure you hire experienced staff. Join a consortium, providing it's a good one. Go for membership of IATA as soon as possible. Have a bright comfortable office with modern equipment. Our main problems have been late payments on business accounts, difficulty in finding suitable staff, 'giveaways' and low deposits by competitors. The plusses have included increasing the turnover, arranging many more tailor-made and long-haul holidays, customer loyalty, and the opportunity for educational visits for myself and staff. (*former secretary, whose agency has three branches in the Midlands*)

> We have a town centre position with a good passing trade and are building a client base across the range from cruising to Benidorm. We have enjoyed selling dreams, and the happiness they give, but it has been difficult adapting to the use of computers. Take care to select a good, prominent site. (*former sales representative in the building industry, Greater Manchester*)

> We took over this agency when it was in a very run-down

state. We set ourselves a five-year target for annual turnover, which we achieved in three and a half years, and by the end of the fifth year we have exceeded our target by 35 per cent. The retail travel sector is not a lucrative one, but it has provided my wife and I with a great deal of interest and social activity which we may not otherwise have found. (*former chartered secretary in the motor trade, Surrey*)

Some late starters in travel and tourism embark on new ventures using knowledge and experience acquired in their previous career. Tonie, a former army major, and his wife, Valmai, organise tours to historic battlefields all over the world. They and their Kent-based team of highly qualified guides accompany tours to the sites of such historic encounters as the Battle of the Somme, the Yangtze Incident, Pearl Harbour, the Indian Mutiny and the Zulu War. The company also supplies a range of military heritage collectables, souvenirs and travel items.

BOAT SERVICES

The notion of swapping the rat race for a life spent messing about in boats is probably one that has occurred to many a restless middle-aged wage slave. The idea was so appealing to some contributors that they turned it into a reality. This is what three of them found:

I left the petrochemical industry mainly for health reasons, and decided to do something I have always wanted to do. I run a twice daily canal passenger boat, a 26-footer carrying 12 passengers. Most trips take about four hours, stopping at a canal-side inn for about one and a quarter hours. I love the canal and all the flora and fauna associated with it, and have good relations with the public. The work is seasonal so I need part-time work in winter. I didn't go into this venture to make a lot of money, just to have a great quality of life. So far, so good. (*former piping supervisor, Lancashire*)

I spent 27 years, largely deskbound, working for the family firm in London. Now I run a one-man (and wife) inland boatyard business, maintaining moorings for privately-owned canal and river boats, operating day-hire craft, and offering a range of services to other river users. I have to work very long hours in summer and I am totally tied to the premises for fear of letting down customers. It is a lonely existence in winter. Sometimes it's difficult to get going when there's much to be done but nothing that *must* be done. The main satisfactions are done but nothing that *must* be done. The main satisfactions are working with things that really interest me, having no employees, no travelling, and beautiful and relaxing surroundings; in short an enhanced quality of life. (*former managing director of an engineering company, Leicestershire*)

I already lived on my boat when I was made redundant. I make and sell rope fenders, stainless steel chimneys and related products for narrow boats. As the business has grown I have had to plan my time and energy to use them to best advantage. It is easy to overtire oneself trying to keep stock levels up. It is essentially a poorly paid field with many people moonlighting, but I enjoy working long hours and require little remuneration. For anyone with more commitments than me, it would not be viable. (*former engineering design draughtsman, Hertfordshire*)

SPORTS COACHING

Many older people who become coaches have previously been involved in sport at a fairly high performance level, but this is not an essential prerequisite. Excellent coach training courses are available for those with an adequate level of fitness and dedication, and there is a shortage of coaches in some sports.

To coach professionally you may need to get an appropriate qualification from your chosen sport's governing body, but generally there is no age barrier. Potential employers include local authorities, private companies and clubs. It may also be possible to get seasonal work at holiday resorts and in leisure centres.

If you are not currently involved in a sport, a useful starting point for information and contacts is the National Coaching Foundation (NCF), which provides courses, resource materials and information for coaches whatever their sport or level of experience. The NCF stresses that the most important quality you need as a coach is enthusiasm. Maturity and life experience are also assets, as are good communication and organisational skills. To help people realise their performance potential, you need to know how the mind and body works and how people respond to exercise and competition.

Other possibilities for mature sports enthusiasts are refereeing and sports administration. Contact the Sports Council or the Scottish Sports Council for further information.

THE HOSPITALITY BUSINESS

An attractive option

Running a hotel, pub or restaurant is probably one of the more frequently occuring notions among middle-agers casting round for a change of career, location and lifestyle. Many attracted to this field prefer either to train for pub management or, if they can raise the capital, invest in a tenancy or run a hotel or restaurant business of their own.

For those looking for jobs rather than a business of their own, most of the work available in the hotel and catering industry and the licensed trade available to people without relevant experience or training tends to be at a fairly junior level with correspondingly modest pay. Jobcentres 'catering' specifically for hotel and catering staff are located in London and a number of other cities. If you have experience in management, sales, marketing or a similar field, you could try approaching one or two of the leading hotel groups direct rather than waiting for suitable job vacancies to be advertised.

Apart from a brief consideration of the opportunities in pub management, this section is directed primarily at those with aspirations to acquire their own business.

Public houses

Over-40s interested in becoming publicans are likely to find a sympathetic ear at the breweries, because maturity is considered a definite plus factor, as is previous business experience.

However, any enquirer who perceives the life of a licensee as a gentle canter spent jollying along the regulars, totting up the profits and having a long lie in in the mornings will be quickly disabused. Running a pub successfully is not only a tough, demanding job, but a way of life, imposing long hours and requiring absolute commitment. The British Institute of Innkeeping (BII) stresses that licensees must know how to market their services, be able to devise new ideas to attract customers, and be familiar with such areas as book-keeping, licensing laws, hygiene, staff motivation, cellar management, merchandising and advertising. A publican's personality as well as his management skills can have a major impact on business. These views were echoed by the late starting publicans I heard from, who included ex-school teachers, a general manager in the motor trade, a Church of England priest and a Scotland Yard detective.

Newcomers must be prepared to adapt to a business that has been changing rapidly in the past few years with the introduction of flexible hours and major investment by the brewers in their premises and the services offered. Alongside the traditional town and country pubs there are now theme pubs, entertainment pubs, pubs with restaurants, disco bars, café bars, steak bars, carveries, and more.

Courses to help build the skills needed to run a pub successfully are provided by the BII and the Hotel, Catering and Institutional Management Association (HCIMA), and training is available at local further education colleges. Another popular option is a two-week residential course at the Brewers' Society training establishment near Shaftesbury in Dorset.

If you have sufficient capital you can take the independent route and buy a free house, but most newcomers have to settle for either a tenancy or managership with a brewery. As a tenant you are your own boss, but you need some capital to purchase the tenancy. You may have difficulty getting taken on by a brewery as a trainee manager after 50, but the age limit is generally a little more flexible for tenancies.

To find out more about career possibilities contact a brewery or the Brewers' Society. Information on tenancy can be obtained from the National Licensed Victuallers Association (NLVA), the Scottish Licensed Trade Association (SLTA), or the Brewers' Society; the NLVA and the SLTA will advise on free house ownership. For both tenancies and free houses you can also get useful advice from a licensed property broker.

WELL, I HAD TO START SOMEWHERE!

Hotels

Most middle-agers who become hoteliers — and these generally tend to be couples — at least begin with some useful credentials, conferred by all those years of being involved in the management of a household, cooking, paying the bills, doing a few running repairs, and entertaining guests. If they have picked up a little business experience along the way as well, that is a positive bonus.

While late starters often build successful business without any formal training, many advocate the wisdom of trying to get some hands-on experience or attending a basic training course, preferably both, before taking the plunge. Courses such as those offered by HCIMA provide a sound preparation.

How do middle-aged beginners fare as hoteliers? Here is what some of them found:

> The three previous owners had given up after only a few months as it was not a viable enterprise. We began with a staff of two full-time and three part-time. My wife did the housekeeping and much of the cooking. I did the reception, the bookings and the billings, and I cleaned the shoes that were left outside bedroom doors. I bought one of those do-it-yourself account books and made a mess of it, but somehow we all muddled through. Now we have 40 staff including part-timers. (*former director of an engineering firm; three star hotel, Cornwall*)

> We took in guests from France and America to see if we liked it before buying our hotel. Our main problem was not having enough capital when we hit bleak times. (*former housewife; small hotel, Devon*)

> We took over a full hotel with only a week's instruction from the vendors. I'm convinced there must be two people involved in running a hotel, but never two couples in partnership. We have seen that formula fall apart many times. Be sure you can do any job in the hotel so your staff can't hold you to ransom. (*former architectural assistant; three star hotel, Cornwall*)

> Both of us enjoyed entertaining and decided to capitalise on our expertise in cooking. One problem was getting used to being 'on the go' 16 hours a day, seven days a week. (*former general manager in the motor trade; 17th century inn, Clwyd*)

Restaurants

Some latecomers to the restaurant trade try to arrange a period of hands-on experience or take a course before setting up on their own, but most seem to settle for learning by observation, trial and error and the application of common sense.

One of those who found success without training, though it wasn't easy, was Jean, a housewife who bought a run-down gift shop in a West Yorkshire tourist town and worked on the premises for 10 months before opening a café. 'I was 53 then,' she recalled. 'I had no catering or business experience, no contacts, and I didn't know where to get anything from, never mind how much I needed. I didn't know anything, only that I wanted to open a smart place. My husband left me in the first year, in the second the VATman was after me for £4500, and my husband wanted paying out for his share in the place. That was just over five years ago, and the venture has proved the best thing I ever did in my life. With no training whatsoever, only flair and determination, and full of zest to be successful, I would say I've got the best café in this town, and there are about ten others close by.'

A different niche in the market was chosen by Brian, a former senior executive with a firm manufacturing mechanical handling equipment, who 'retired' himself at 43 and bought a restaurant in a small Somerset town. He took with him 'no expertise, only great enthusiasm' and built a business with a nationally recognised standard of cooking and wine cellar. He won a string of prestigious food awards and inclusion in leading food and wine guides, and at its peak his list included some 500 different wines. In his spare moments he found time to write a book on wine; this proved so successful that he subsequently leased his restaurant to concentrate full-time on writing, broadcasting, lecturing and judging.

Catering business

A number of over-40s have applied their cookery and organisational skills to setting up businesses which handle catering for functions such as conferences, office parties and weddings. This kind of business can be run from home, but a well-equipped kitchen with adequate freezer or larder storage space are necessary. In addition to the food, and in some cases beverages, you must be prepared to provide crockery and cutlery, and such items as ash trays and candlesticks.

Maturity should be a help in winning business, providing it is combined with a flair for preparing tasty food and presenting it well.

Home economist

Experience built up in running a home for several years can be usefully applied by the middle-ager in a career as a home economist, not only in the hotel and catering industry but on the staff of, say, a food manufacturer, school or public utility such as a gas or electricity board, or in the social services.

To work as a professional adviser in this field you will normally need specialist training to higher national diploma or degree level. Mature students are welcomed on the courses and may be admitted without the customary minimum academic qualifications.

Toastmaster

Toastmasters officiate at events ranging from weddings and rugby club dinners to civic balls and royal banquets. They are often called upon to advise on and sometimes take charge of the organisation of events, including choosing the foods, wines, entertainment and venue.

Maturity is an undoubted plus factor in this profession, but other qualities are also needed, such as a good, clear voice, confidence, an assuring presence and calmness under pressure.

Many of the top flight toastmasters have trained at the school for professional toastmasters run by Ivor Spencer, who has officiated at over 1000 royal events during nearly 40 years in the business. Ivor, who left school at 14 and began his career as a trainee chef, has become a celebrity in his own right through his work in the UK and other countries as a toastmaster, trainer of toastmasters, master of ceremonies, after dinner speaker, lecturer and writer.

One of Ivor's protégés, Robert, who trained as a toastmaster after being made redundant at 50 from his job as personnel manager with a food company, said it was obvious from observing untrained toastmasters that formal training was essential for a professional performance. Success needs dedication, he added, and the idea that just because you have a big voice you can become a good master of ceremonies is misinformed.

Other relevant information will be found in the section 'Butler' in chapter 10.

THE AD SAID — STAFF WANTED FOR LEISURE WORK

10

Personal Services

BEAUTY AND GROOMING

Beauty therapy

For a career as a beauty therapist maturity can be a considerable asset. A spokesman for the International Health and Beauty Council, one of the industry's main educational bodies, said a large percentage of clients in beauty salons are over 40 and tend to welcome therapists of similar age to whom they can relate more easily. He added that older women entering beauty therapy 'do not always realise how much information they have about the functioning of human bodies, physical problems and solutions, arising from their own experience and observation. This gives them a head start over younger students.' The mature entrants who achieve greatest success are often those who set up their own salons or who concentrate on home visiting.

A variety of full-time and part-time courses leading to qualifications in beauty therapy and related work are available both at specialist schools and further education colleges. The subjects taught include cosmetics, body massage, hair grooming, slimming techniques, electrolysis, fashion, make-up, manicure and skin treatments. Training establishments may waive standard entry requirements for mature students.

In addition to beauty therapists, others working in the field include beauticians, who perform a somewhat narrower range of procedures, and beauty consultants, who are generally employed by a cosmetic or perfume manufacturer.

Hairdressing/trichology

Some hairdressers train entirely on-the-job, others attend courses, such as City and Guilds, at local further education colleges or specialist schools.

Once trained, you have a number of options. You can work for an established business, open your own salon, work at home, or become an itinerant hairdresser visiting clients in their own homes. With growing numbers of both women and men having their hair treated, styled and set on a regular basis, the income can be fairly high if you are prepared to put in the hours at times convenient to your customers. Remember, though, it is tiring work as you are on your feet most of the time.

According to the Hairdressing Training Board, the industry welcomes people of all ages for training and no formal qualifications are needed. The Board offers this advice to mature entrants from other occupations: 'The skills and experience you have gained will be assessed and credited towards an NVQ (national vocational qualification) at the level best suited to your abilities and a training programme worked out for your own personal needs. Employment training (ET) offers funding towards an NVQ, or there is the possibility of a career development loan.'

Christine, a former private secretary who, at 43, bought an existing hairdressing business in Lothian, Scotland, learned from her staff and through a day release course at a local further education college. She now has two salons, doing both ladies' and men's hairdressing and catering mainly for a middle-aged clientele. She and her staff of ten see most of their clients by regular appointment, with little passing trade. 'One of the problems is difficulty in getting staff due to the long hours and hard work involved.' said Christine. 'There is generally a high level of drop-outs by apprentices in the first year, but I find that if they survive that year they go on to finish their training. Most of my girls have been with me since leaving school. A big threat to business is the growing number of mobile salons, because they can offer lower charges.'

A number of hairdressers qualify to practise trichology, the treatment of disorders of the hair and scalp. The Institute of Trichologists, which offers training, told me that several of its students each year are over 40. The two-year course, completed mainly by correspondence, covers such subjects as anatomy and physiology, organic and inorganic chemistry, and nutrition, as well as a range of topics directly concerned with the hair and scalp.

DRIVING SERVICES

Driving instructor

Although it can sometimes be a 'heart in the mouth' occupation there appears to be no shortage of middle-agers keen to get on the road as driving instructors. Driving schools have proliferated in the past decade, more than a few of them set up by men and women made redundant or taking early retirement. Apart from maturity, they frequently bring to the job many years of experience behind the wheel, and perhaps have taught members of their family or friends to drive.

Success as a professional instructor requires such qualities as patience, alertness, and the ability to get along with people of varying backgrounds and temperament. It is also necessary to pass an examination set by the Department of Transport and be placed on the Register of Approved Driving Instructors (ADI) maintained by the Department. Before taking the qualifying exam candidates must have held a full driving licence for at least four years and be assessed as a 'fit and proper person', taking into account both motoring and any other offences which might be on their record. The examination consists of a written paper and ability tests in both driving and instruction. Information on the ADI test can be obtained from the Driving Standards Agency.

Most driving instructors are self-employed, but those seeking employment with established driving schools may find that some have an upper age limit of 45.

Here is a representative selection of comments from contributors, whose previous occupations include sales executive, teacher, police traffic patrol officer, housewife and oil industry worker:

> The satisfactions of the job include watching clients develop from raw beginner to passing the test, seeing their joy and gratitude when they pass, and meeting former pupils out on the road.

> I found it relatively easy to qualify, and the capital outlay and risk low. I work from home and my wife helps with the books, telephone, etc. Building up custom is a fairly slow process and it can take up to 18 months to become established.

> Driving instruction is a crowded field, and to make a decent living it is necessary work long hours, including weekends. I moved to Wales to 'retire' and decided to take up driving instruction as a paid hobby. I qualified and opened my own school when I was 60. I took further exams and am now what is called a Diamond Instructor.

Driving examiner

The Ministry of Transport is prepared to consider well-qualified candidates up to the age of 50 for posts as driving examiners. Applicants need to have held a driving licence for six years and are required to take part in a competitive examination. This involves an interview, driving test and a four-week course followed by a special test.

The Ministry examiners look for such qualities as patience, tact, unflappability and an air of authority.

Taxi driver

Cab driving is often a second career, but to qualify as a licensed taxi driver you have to pass fairly searching written and practical tests, which vary according to the local authority concerned. Most taxi drivers are self-employed though they may hire their cab from a company either on a rental or 'cut of takings' basis. The work can involve long and unsocial hours, and the size of income will depend on the number of hours put in.

An alternative option, if you have a four-door car and a clean driving licence, is to become a mini-cab driver. You are self-employed and able to work hours to suit yourself. You get business by paying rent to a mini-cab company, which handles requests from the public for cabs and passes them on to its members. Unlike licensed taxis, mini-cabs cannot ply for hire on the streets.

Chauffeur/chauffeuse

You could put your years of driving experience to profitable use as a chauffeur or chauffeuse for a private employer, business or industrial company, or in the public sector.

Training courses are run by some of the larger driving schools.

EMPLOYMENT AGENCY/CAREERS ADVISER

Varied work experience and contacts in business and industry are valuable assets which the middle-ager can bring to the operation of an employment agency or work as a careers adviser.

Audrey, whose previous career included spells in nursing, administration, training, product promotion and public relations, made use of her working background to establish a successful employment agency in the north-east. 'The response to my initial advertisement was enormous,' she said. 'In a very short time I had a variety of people on my list from home helps, cleaners and cooks to engineers, script writers and graphic artists. I interviewed them all in their homes. Then I decided that the only way to project myself and let the employers know about the time and money they could save by referring to my list of hand picked staff was to go knocking on their doors and meet them face to face. I found welcome encouragement for my venture, and became involved in business projects with staff working not only in the UK but internationally.'

Some achieve success with agencies specially geared to utilising the talents of older work seekers. For example, a firm called *Grey Matters* found success by specialising in the placement of men and women over 45, while models from the 1950s and 1960s including Tania Mallet, who starred in the James Bond film *Goldfinger*, got together to form a modelling agency, *Déjà Vu*, for the over-40s.

Careers advisers work in a variety of settings, from large corporations and universities to independent consultancies. In addition to wide experience in business, industry or the public service, it is also valuable to have some acquaintance with psychology and counselling. Practitioners should also be well versed in such matters as interview skills and the preparation of effective CVs.

Posts in careers offices based at local authorities throughout the country provide challenging opportunities to help young people find or change careers, and many of the offices also offer adult guidance services. A specialist one-year course is offered at the Kent College for the Careers Service at Swanley. To qualify for entry you need a degree or two years relevant experience.

INTRODUCTION AGENCY

Middle-agers who open introduction agencies may start with the advantage of maturity and life experience, but sound business experience can be just as important.

The casualty rate of new businesses in this field is high, with some agencies opening and closing in a matter of weeks. The Association of British Introduction Agencies said that the main reason for this appears to be that, although most people start with the best of intentions, they have insufficient business acumen or resources to sustain them. It has been estimated that funding of £6000 to £10000 is needed to start up even a modest enterprise, with advertising being one of the major expenditure items.

The principal of a London marriage bureau and a member of the Society of Marriage Bureaux told me, 'Having taken over an existing bureau at the age of 46, I would advise anyone entering the field to be extremely careful. It is a huge undertaking, emotionally and financially. To set up a bureau from nothing would, I suspect, be immensely difficult. One of the biggest problems, even for an established bureau, is that in the 40 + age group, and more severely in the 50 + , there is a growing imbalance in the number of men and women — masses more women seeking marriage and remarriage than men, and men wanting to meet someone significantly younger than themselves.'

ESCORT AGENCY

Another employment possibility which some gregarious individuals might wish to explore is that provided by escort agencies. Such enterprises, like massage parlours, have sometimes had a bad press through the activities of a few dubious operators, but there are many perfectly respectable firms, some of which employ older people.

If this kind of work appeals, you could contact a few agencies (see the *Yellow Pages*) and ask if they use mature people on a freelance basis. You would, of course, be expected to be personable, presentable, patient, reasonably articulate and happy to work in the evenings.

BUTLER

Your maturity will be an asset if you aspire to become a butler, but, according to Ivor Spencer, a leading authority on the profession, you will also need discretion, loyalty, integrity, an ability to get on with everyone and a low-key manner.

Ivor runs courses for butlers in England and the United States, and his protégés serve in households around the world, including those of royalty, business tycoons and Hollywood stars. During the intensive six-week courses offered by the Ivor Spencer International School in Surrey and New York for Butler Administrators/ Personal Assistants, men (and occasionally women) are trained to take responsibility for such matters as purchasing and caring for food, wines and cigars, arranging menus, planning and running functions such as parties and barbeques, hiring staff, looking after clothes and booking travel for their employers. They are taught how to be the epitome of tact and courtesy, and become 'a friend of the family, a confidante, and an uncle-like figure to the children.' Ivor takes students from 17 to 60, but warns applicants that female butlers are not easy to place.

See also the section on 'Toastmaster' in chapter 9.

CHILDMINDING

Childminding in your own home is an option to consider if you enjoy looking after young children. Local authorities have a statutory obligation to consider all applications for registration as a childminder, and, for the price of a stamped addressed envelope, you can also get helpful advice from the National Childminding Association.

FUNERAL WORK

Maturity, tact, a sympathetic manner and a driving licence are useful credentials for a job in the funeral business. The work can involve driving, pall bearing and assisting with administrative work. To find out more, check the *Yellow Pages* for funeral directors in your area, and give one or two of them a discreet call.

GENEALOGY

Many genealogists enter the profession in their mature years, sometimes getting 'hooked' as a result of researching their own family trees. No formal qualifications are required, but considerable know-how has to be accumulated to do work on a professional basis.

If you are interested, start by reading any books you can find on the subject in your local library, and familiarise yourself with vital sources of information like parish records and other reference material in libraries and museums. It is well worth joining a family history society if you have one in your area, and also the Society of Genealogists, which produces a magazine, sponsors lectures and courses, and offers access to their excellent library and collection of historical materials. Also, if you can't already, learn to type.

The Association of Genealogists and Record Agents (AGRA), advised that many of its members derive only part of their living from genealogical work and many have built up their practices slowly while working in other professions. To qualify for full membership of AGRA you need considerable professional experience, and must produce satisfactory evidence of this, including samples of work. However, newcomers can become affiliates of the Association with the backing of two acceptable referees.

After being made redundant from his job as a brewers' representative, Joseph decided to research his family history. He became fascinated by the subject and built up his knowledge through research and reading and courses in genealogy offered by the Workers Educational Association. He then began tracing ancestors in the north-east for clients both in the UK and several overseas countries, and has become increasingly busy. His work involves compiling pedigree charts using such sources as parish and non-conformist registers, census returns, civil registrations, wills and many lesser known records. 'There are no short cuts,' he said. 'Integrity, patience, persistence and hard work are essential. One can be a successful genealogist without taking any courses; aptitude is the higher priority.'

GRAPHOLOGY

While graphology, the study of handwriting to determine character and personality, arouses scepticism in some quarters, it is used by many businesses in Britain and elsewhere as an aid to assessing job applicants and staff.

A considerable proportion of professional graphologists enter the field after 40. Lawrence Warner, director of the UK-based International Graphoanalysis Society, said that the bulk of students taking courses through the society's tutorial service were between 40 and 50. Properly trained, qualified graphoanalysts can earn a good living, he added, and the single European market is expected to give the discipline a boost because of its wide use in several EC countries.

HELPING HAND SERVICES

If you are practical, resourceful, and enjoy a challenge, you could consider starting a 'helping hand' service. Examples of successful operations of this kind are those run by *Universal Aunts, Homesitters Limited* and *Motivity*.

Universal Aunts look after children, pets or property, book hotels, supply domestic staff, arrange programmes for business entertaining, do shopping, decorate houses, witness marriages, find the unobtainable, and carry out a myriad of other tasks. The majority of universal aunts — and uncles — are recruited from the over-40 age group.

The aims of the service provided by Homesitters Limited are to protect homes from burglars, squatters and vandals; reduce the chore of 'shutting up the house', and save the owners the cost and worry of putting their pets into kennels by letting them remain in familiar surroundings. The work provides the homesitter (who may take a partner) with the chance to enjoy a regular change of scene and earn a little money as well. To qualify as a homesitter you have to be 'mature, responsible and over 40', and provide reliable references going back over 20 years. The firm has no lack of applicants and is very selective.

Motivity describes itself as the 'oddest job people' who specialise in the jobs no-one else wants to do. Tasks they have been set include providing 500 corpses for a horror film, coming up with 150 clean riddles, and painting 200 human glass eyes to look bloodshot!

11

Creating and Performing

THE VISUAL ARTS

Ingredients of success

Whatever medium the creative artist chooses, there is no surefire recipe for success, but demonstrably the most important ingredient is talent. To this should be added liberal quantities of hard work and determination, and a sprinkling of luck.

Most contributors who have made their mark as artists agree that the rewards for success are not just financial; they include such things as the sheer enjoyment of creation, the satisfaction of acquiring new skills, the opportunity to decide your own work schedule, and the thrill of seeing your work published or displayed by clients. Not all contributors attended formal training courses, but most spent some years honing their skills as amateurs before devoting themselves full-time to art. Many evolved distinctive styles or specialised in particular media or subjects, and generally started selling work before making their hobby their business.

The following examples show how some over-40s made their mark in the art world.

Animal magic

Although she enjoyed her work as a primary school teacher in Portsmouth, June felt the need for a change of direction after her family had grown up and left home. So, at the age of 52, she decided to try and convert her hobby of painting into a profession. The living room of her home became her studio and gradually she began to attract commissions. A particularly strong demand developed for her studies of animals, a speciality she had evolved as an amateur artist.

From the outset she adopted a businesslike approach, keeping a careful record of all outgoings and receipts. She had her accounts audited and reported her income to the tax inspector, although in that first year she was not liable to tax. As well as keeping a record of work done, she also photographs it and keeps an album. This is useful because 99 per cent of her work is commissioned or sold.

'As a self-employed person, it is essential to work as if you are employed by someone else,' she said. 'Do not fritter time away, and beware of interruptions. The telephone is a mixed blessing. Allow time for book-keeping, filing and keeping records up to date. I found pricing work difficult at first, but I worked out a scale related to sizes, media and frames. Sometimes would-be clients gasp at my prices, expecting something virtually for nothing, while others are surprised at the reasonable charge, so I suppose I have pitched it about right. I gradually put up my prices by a percentage that enables me to cope not only with inflation, but keeps demand for my work at a rate I can manage.'

Flying start

Many sales of his paintings as an amateur enabled Paul, a former Westminster City Council official, to make a flying start as an artist after he decided to quit his job because of high blood pressure. In his first year he sold £18,000 worth of paintings and has never looked back.

Aged 42 and married with three children when he made the break, he told me, 'I grew up in an artistic home environment and have drawn and sketched all my life. My subject is landscape and latterly has developed into atmospheric landscape. Early on I started painting from imagination and now about 80 per cent of my landscapes are imaginary.'

Paul's work is handled by galleries throughout Britain and he has several one-man exhibitions each year. His paintings are in collections in several countries.

Success in miniature

At the age of 42 Bill gave up a highly paid job as regional director of an international group of American advertising agencies in Asia to return to the UK and devote himself to portrait and miniature painting.

He established his home and studio in his native Berkshire. 'Word of mouth was the only way I gained commissions,' he said, 'and things were a bit slow at first. Obviously I had to accept a much lower income that I was earning in advertising.' Everything changed after he won the BP Exhibit of the Year Award at the Royal Academy, and today his work is in royal, public and private collections in every continent.

Bill paints his miniatures in water colour on ivory, and occasionally on vellum, using the finest sable brushes available to achieve the most intricate detail possible. Large portraits are painted in oils or water colour.

Persistence pays off

Turning to painting as therapy following a nervous breakdown caused by the ending of her marriage led Janet, a former primary school teacher, into a professional artistic career at the age of 41.

To her surprise she sold her first two canvasses immediately, but after that her attempts to get her work accepted 'involved endless hours walking round the galleries,' but she was 'absolutely determined not to give up.' Her persistence eventually paid off and within two years she was exhibiting her work at important London galleries. She is widely collected, and her paintings have frequently been reproduced as limited edition prints and cards.

For other talented painters of mature years with professional aspirations, Janet had this advice: 'Don't give up. There are people who will recognise what you do. You must find them. The key word is work.'

Check list:

- Don't quit the day job until your work is selling regularly.
- Be persistent in promoting yourself to galleries and potential clients.
- Be businesslike.

CONSERVATION

After a career developing new products for a leading soup company, Stephen, a chemist, decided at 43 to follow up his lifelong interest in art by becoming a conservationist and restorer. A particular attraction of conservation work was that it provided an opportunity to combine art and technical skills.

His former employers agreed to finance the first year of a two-year Masters degree in art conservation run by Gateshead Technical College in conjunction with the University of Northumbria. Competition for places was strong and the course was demanding, covering such subjects as practical conservation, history of materials, artists' techniques, chemistry, physics and art history. Students ranged in age from early twenties to 46.

After graduating, the main difficulty Stephen faced was getting known in a specialist field, and establishing credibility so that institutions would trust him with valuable works of art. Most newly qualified conservators work with experienced practitioners or large museums, but he was self-employed from the outset, and he has found the experience enjoyable. 'Conservation work does not seem like work,' he said.

DESIGN

Whether working in graphic, textile, fashion, three-dimensional or any other branch of design, the designer has to combine creative ability with technical knowledge. While it is possible to develop the necessary skills without formal training, most take courses, usually at degree or diploma level.

After graduating at 44 from a four-year course in graphic design, former school teacher Vanetta found that potential employers were reluctant to take on someone of her age and were unwilling to entrust the more responsible assignments to an artist so newly qualified and inexperienced. 'I broke into the graphic design business by doing work for Oxfam and other local charity organisations to gain experience and get printed work for a portfolio,' she said. 'Eventually I got some other commissions by writing targeted letters to editors, personnel officers, etc. of companies within a 30-miles radius of home.' The breakthrough to regular work came when she obtained a commission from a local publishing firm, and was able to establish an ongoing contact with an editor. 'Get a sound training,' advised Vanetta, 'a piece of paper always helps. Be persistent, polite, not a pest when looking for commissions. Establish personal working relationships with commissioning editors.'

At 55, Wanda and her husband, then 60, set up a partnership to produce designs for industrial printed fabrics. Wanda, a former occupational therapist with a diploma in graphic design, works at the drawing board and he handles the other aspects of the business. 'My husband has retired, so it's more enjoyable to work at home on a project together,' she said. 'It is a case of learning from scratch. No capital risk is involved and we have enough income to work on a speculative basis. I was always interested in repeat pattern, and it is proving fun. This could be a good field for those with lots of drive and enterprise, experience at selling themselves, and love of repeat design.'

After 20 years at home bringing up three children, Jenny decided to follow up her long-standing interest in sculpture and model making by taking an honours degree in interior design, specialising in 3-D design at the University of Teesside. 'I did O and A levels before starting the degree, but a "foundation" year at an art school would have been even more useful for my particular course,' she said. 'I enjoyed nearly all aspects of the course, and eventually learned to be pushier about my work, but needed a lot of encouragement.' She now works with her husband, a land resources manager, doing designs for conversions of barns and other buildings.

CRAFTS

Craft industries

Many successful craftsmen and women have developed their businesses from a hobby, and the skills necessary to earn a reasonable living can be acquired later in life.

Success in a craft industry depends primarily on the quality of the product, but it also requires hard work, enthusiasm and business acumen, whether you are selling direct to the public, the retail trade or exporting. It is important to study the products of others in the same field, and to try to offer something a little different. Some of the most successful workers are those who find a niche in the market and meet the demand with high quality products.

The many craft fairs held regularly around the country offer useful outlets, even for those who sell from their own premises. Some craftsmen and women also sell a proportion of their output by mail order, attracting business by advertising in carefully selected publications.

Courses in most of the more popular crafts, such as pottery, basketry and embroidery, are offered at adult education centres as well as specialist colleges. A number of firms supply kits containing the materials you need to develop your skills at home.

Ceramics

Ceramics is among the more popular media, and offers a wide range of specialities, ranging from the production of decorative pots to the crafting of dolls. There is no formal apprentice scheme for on-the-job training as a potter, but some established craftsmen and women are prepared to take on assistants and teach them the basic techniques. Setting up in business involves a fairly substantial outlay on equipment, and subsequent rewards may be more in terms of job satisfaction than high earnings.

Basketry

Several contributors who trained in basketry are using their skills to help meet the continuing demand for well-crafted products.

Thomas went from Scotland to take a course in willow basketmaking at West Dean College, Sussex, after hearing about it on a television holiday programme. He began by making baskets for relatives and friends, and then moved on to selling at car boot sales and craft fairs. 'Making a living from basketry can mean long hours,' he said. 'We are competing with imports from Taiwan and Hong Kong, although their products are often shoddy compared to ours.'

Forced to give up her London medical practice due to ill health, Sandra retrained in chair restoration and seating. She attended adult education classes and weekend courses with the Basketry Association, and also worked with an experienced craftsman in his chair workshop. After operating from home for three years she bought a shop in Cumbria with residential accommodation, a workshop and retail area. There she makes and sells rush, cane, skeined willow, cord and seagrass seating, restores chair frames, and buys chairs at auction for restoration and sale.

Antique restoration

Restoring beautiful objects is arguably one of life's more satisfying pursuits, and it can provide a good living if you have the necessary talent and skills. It is a field that attracts many older people, and they are generally well represented on the appropriate training courses.

Simon, a former British Airways helicopter pilot who had to give up flying at 50 for medical reasons, took a one-year full-time course in antique clock restoration at West Dean College, Sussex. 'I enjoyed the course and the relaxed life, and the opportunity to meet people eminent in the horological field was very valuable,' he said. 'However the course was too short, so I worked until 10 pm every night to get the most out of it. I anticipate it will take a year or so to get the restoration business established. I equipped my workshop at home while I still had a salary. It's probably necessary to deal as well as restore, so some flair in this area is helpful. It is even more labour intensive than furniture restoration, and long hours are unavoidable.'

Other middle-aged West Dean students I heard from were a computer salesman and an engineering lecturer who both trained in furniture restoration, and a redundant sales executive who took the antique clock restoration course.

Thatching
For those with a head for heights, the traditional country craft of thatching offers a good living once the necessary skills have been acquired.

Edwin, a former tenant farmer in Devon, entered the trade at the age of 60 after he had earlier learned to thatch by trial and error when he had difficulty in finding a thatcher to fix the roof of his farm. His first client was a neighbour, more contracts soon followed, and eventually he was booked up two years ahead. 'You are never too old to learn,' he told me, 'but in this work you must be very adaptable, have strong hands and arms, and not mind the weather, which can be very rough at times. No two roofs are alike, but it gets easier with experience and application of common sense. The worst problems are in built-up areas from traffic and smoke of all sorts of chimneys. I was fortunate in that both my father and grandfather were builders because a thatcher has to know something about walls and carpentry, and have a straight eye.'

The Thatching Advisory Service will provide information on training, and also tell you about its popular franchising system.

Other options
Among the many other options available to those attracted by a career in crafts are spinning and weaving, wood carving, hedging and walling, making rakes and besoms, toymaking, knitting, patchwork and glovemaking.

CHECK LIST

- Aim to produce top quality products.
- Explore niche markets: try to provide something that others don't.
- Business acumen is important as most craft workers are self-employed.

CREATIVE WRITING

Starting late

Most professional fiction writers began as part-time amateurs, fitting in their writing around their 'day jobs'.

The fact that so many writers start their careers in middle-age has been acknowledged by the establishment of an award, the *McKitterick Prize*, administered by the Society of Authors for a first novel by an author over 40. Whatever your age, however, success in creative writing requires both hard work and talent. Few writers achieve publication before first having tasted rejection, sometimes repeatedly.

Novels

One lady had the manuscript of her novel returned without a covering letter, but with these words written across the back page in red ink: 'Strongly advise author not to take up writing as a career.' She wept and stopped writing for a fortnight; then she gritted her teeth and began again. Her name: Catherine Cookson, whose powerful, heart-warming novels have sold in their millions around the world.

Catherine, whose first novel was published when she was 43, is encouraging to other aspiring writers. 'You must first of all make up your mind,' she said, 'to turn deaf ears to all those well-wishers who tell you the markets are swamped already and that there isn't a hope in hell for newcomers; or that — take their word for it — there's no money in this game.'

She remembers how she left the north-east of England when she was 22, taking one suitcase with her, 'but a great deal of mental luggage' concerning the people she had known and the experiences of her younger days. 'It wasn't until I realised that I had brought with me from my early environment all the material I would ever need for my stories that I wrote my first novel — and real story — and so came into my own,' she said. 'If you want to touch the heart of a reader, and I think this should be the aim of the writer, then write about the kind of people you know from the inside, whether your acquaintance with them was in the slums, in the middle class, or in a stately home, because then, and only then, will you get your heart into your work. And that is what your reader wants, that is what holds the reader, that is what makes one reader say to another those beautiful words: I couldn't put it down.'

Two other best-selling writers who found success in middle age, Anita Burgh and Maeve Binchy, also had words of encouragement for late starters.

Anita, who began writing at 45 and had her first novel published when she was 50, advised, 'Never give up. Listen to criticism and advice. I talk to quite a lot of writers' groups and I hear failed writers complaining that the publisher or the agents were stupid not to recognise how good their book is, or were so presumptuous to advise re-writing. I always say *listen to them*. If they don't publish it's because it isn't good enough; any book can always be made better. Regard rejections as a challenge. Say "I will make it better, I'll show them." even when your heart is breaking.

Don't show your work to your best friend and relations; they will undoubtedly tell you it is marvellous rather than hurt your feelings. Pace yourself. At 50 one cannot rush around on a promotional tour quite how your PR firm would like, you have to learn to say "no". Have confidence in yourself. This is perhaps the hardest hurdle. Just because you are at home scribbling you require as much confidence and faith in yourself as if you had, in middle age, taken a job in an office or shop with all the adjustments that requires. Resign yourself to the fact that no-one will take you seriously as a writer until you are published. You have to grow another skin against cynicism. Tell yourself every day "I can do it."'

Irish novelist Maeve Binchy achieved international success with such novels as *Light a Penny Candle, Firefly Summer* and *The Copper Beech*. When I asked her to what she attributed her relatively late breakthrough as a best selling author, she told me, 'I think the secret, if there is one, is that I had met a lot of people, seen a lot of life and was a bit more mature than youngsters, and therefore able to judge what was worthy and what was not. Also I knew you had to keep a steady job and not go mad for the sake of art. The practicality of being middle-aged is useful — also we are used to things not always turning out well and we do not die of grief over failure. I put in six hours work five days a week at a typewriter. I sit down and will not get up until those hours are over, so it's easier to write the damn thing than to look at it.'

Many others who started and made their breakthrough to writing success in middle age — more than a few with romantic fiction — sent me contributions. Here is a brief representative selection of their advice and comments:

Your age is immaterial — your work is judged on its merits.

Previously I had sublimated the creative urge in the process of having children and bringing them up.

I knew I had found the ideal occupation to augment the family income as painlessly as possible.

Write about what you know; it's the quality of the canvas that matters, not the size.

Read the type of things you want to write, but don't copy.

Thoroughly research your market; make sure you send your manuscript to a publisher who handles the type of story you have written.

My first book was written, rejected and rewritten at least six times before it appeared in print.

Everything I have written so far has been accepted by someone.

Don't be put off by people saying you must have an agent to get published. I had my first two books published without one, but do get one when you can.

Poetry

For most people who write poetry it is inevitably a labour of love. As Robert Graves put it, 'There is no money in poetry, but then there is no poetry in money.' To stand a chance of being commercially viable, a book of poetry usually has to have a well-known name on the cover.

If you enjoy writing poetry, try submitting your work to some of the many small poetry magazines, and enter a few of the regular competitions held each year (public libraries often display leaflets promoting them). For those desperate to see their work in print, there is always the option of self-publishing; a number of poets have chosen this route, although it involves a great deal of work and can be fairly expensive, depending on the type of publication.

Playwriting
Probably the most realistic starting point for the aspiring dramatist is a local drama group or small theatre company. If your work has exceptional merit you might get a sympathetic hearing from a theatre like the Royal Court in London, which presents work by new writers. Another possibility is to enter one of the competitions which offer production of the winner's play.

Many mature playwrights earn their first cheque from BBC Radio and a few manage to sell to BBC Television or one of the ITV companies, though the market for one-off plays on TV has greatly diminished.

Comedy writing
Writing good comedy material is a difficult art, but if you have the flair for it, there are a variety of potential markets. Some newcomers start by sending jokes to stand-up comedians or submitting 'quickies' and sketches for radio and television comedy programmes. If you are able to establish something of a track record, more opportunities could open up, such as scriptwriting for TV and radio situation comedies.

One late starter who made it to the big-time is Eric Chappell, who spent 23 years as an auditor with an electricity board before quitting to take his chances as a full-time playwright. He had an instant hit with his first play, *The Banana Boat* (produced at the Apollo Theatre), and this inspired his first situation comedy for television, the hugely successful *Rising Damp*. Since then he has scripted a string of hits, such as *Only When I Laugh*, *The Bounder*, *Duty Free*, as well as several plays, picking up numerous awards along the way.

Sources of help
You could save a lot of time on trial and error by reading and absorbing some of the excellent 'how to' books on the market. These will take you through the mysteries of plotting, characterisation, markets and other practical considerations, but you have to supply the talent.

Also consider attending one of the helpful writers courses and gatherings held in different parts of the country each year. Among the best are the Writers' Summer School which takes place at Swanwick, Derbyshire, in August, the Writers' Holiday at Caerleon, Gwent, in July, and the regular courses organised by the Arvon Foundation at their centres in Devon, Yorkshire and Inverness.

Joining a local writers circle can be a stimulating antidote to the isolation which is one of the occupational hazards of the writer.

CHECK LIST:

- Write the kind of material you like reading.
- Research your market thoroughly.
- Write something every day.

THE PERFORMING ARTS

What it takes

There have always been actors, musicians, singers and other entertainers who become professionals in their mature years, and a few even find stardom. In a business where maturity won't win you many brownie points, those who make it are likely to have a special combination of talent, stamina and luck. Others who dream of seeing their names in lights often have to settle for something a little more modest by the time they reach 40. Some devote themselves to teaching others what they have learned, or simply indulge their enjoyment of performance by participating in amateur or semi-professional productions.

In many branches of show business, for example stand-up comedy or magic, little formal training is available and the performer learns primarily by experience and observing other professionals at work. An act tends to be developed largely by trial and error. The unknown has to try every potential source of work, from holiday camps and cruise liners to local clubs and residential homes. Talent shows are also worth entering as they can sometimes lead to contracts for work.

Acting

With the majority of its members out of work at any one time, and most of the others making only a precarious living, the acting profession is hardly in need of more recruits, particularly of the older variety. But this is unlikely to put off those determined to tread the boards professionally.

It is not essential to attend a drama school to become a professional actor, but it is becoming increasingly common to do so. The over-40s, however, are likely to find a mixed reception from the top training establishments. The Royal Academy of Dramatic Art (RADA), for example, does not encourage applications from students over 35; the School of Drama at the Royal Scottish

Academy of Music and Drama (RSAMD), on the other hand, sets no upper age limit and has 'a positive interest in recruiting mature students, but not by active discrimination.' It is believed that the oldest drama student accepted at RSAMD was 51.

A number of higher education institutions which offer diploma and degree courses with a significant drama component consider older applicants on their individual merits.

Peter, an engineer and part-time musician, got 'hooked' on drama and gave up his job at 42 to take a creative arts degree at Nottingham Trent University. 'The course was unstructured, but self-motivating,' he told me. 'It was very hard work, mentally and physically draining at times, sometimes having to work 18 hours at a stretch.' During the course Peter had a play on Radio Four and a short film featured on BBC 2. He helped cover his living expenses with work as a television extra, having previously obtained his Equity card (membership of the British Actors Equity Association, the performers' trade union). After graduation Peter intended to continue with both his acting and writing.

A postgraduate diploma course in theatre studies at University College, Cardiff, was the route chosen by Derek, a reference book editor, who wanted to change the direction of his career radically as he entered his forties. 'There were about 15 students on the course,' he said. 'Most were fresh graduates, but a couple of others were around 30. It was a very practical course, and involved putting on a good number of productions in the nine months. When I came to the end of the course, I think I had decided it wasn't really for me. I don't regret doing it. There was much that I enjoyed. I achieved at least one notable acting success. I suppose it fulfilled a fantasy I had long had. I did apply desultorily for some jobs in the field, but I really needed more experience. I would probably have had to take a £6000 a year dogsbody job to get it. My former employers had kept my job open for me, so I went back to that.'

Check list
- Take a good quality drama training course if possible.
- Qualify as soon as you can for Equity membership.
- Be persistent and optimistic.

Singing
Though occasionally a singer finds popular success in mid-life, he or she has usually been singing as an amateur or semi-professional for some years before.

The over-40s are rarely accepted for training at music colleges and academies, but a notable exception was businessman and tenor Roland Sidwell, who obtained a place at the National Opera Studio (NOS) in his forties and later went on to sing principal roles at the English National Opera and the Royal Opera House, Covent Garden. The Director of the NOS told me, 'Except in the case of a very exceptional voice, I would not advise a person to attempt to make such a change so late in life, because they have so much experience to gain before they can expect to fulfil the aspirations commensurate with their age.'

One of those who made it as a popular singer in his forties was Eddie Taylor, who became a vocalist with the String of Pearls Orchestra and other big bands, after retiring from the police service at the age of 47. He has shared the stage on tour with such famous names as Joan Regan and Guy Mitchell, and has done a number of radio recordings as a band singer, as well as appearing at concerts all over the country. Before he began singing in public in his forties, said Eddie, he had 'done nothing remotely like it, apart from giving evidence in court, where one must be a good performer.'

After teaching herself folk guitar and then giving lessons to children at school and in her home, Irene, a former auxiliary teaching assistant, decided to try her luck as an entertainer, singing and playing the guitar. 'I had no contacts in the business,' she said, 'and it was physically tiring, as a small female, lugging around a large amplifier. At my first engagement I did a small spot between choral items at a concert. I was terrified. I felt as if my hands didn't belong to my arms. I have since learned a lot about music of the 20th century, and I feel that my singing and playing are constantly improving. Entertaining the old and handicapped is very rewarding.'

Music

Even with years of experience as an amateur it is difficult to make it as a professional musician after 40, particularly as a solo performer, but some manage it, notably in the popular music field. Virtually all work on a freelance basis.

The route to professional status can sometimes be fairly rapid for the pop musician. With no previous musical knowledge or experience, Jackie played her first gig at 40, just three months after her husband bought her a keyboard. 'He had gone out to buy a drum machine with a view to working around the local pubs as a guitar/vocalist,' she told me. 'When he brought a Casio keyboard home instead and announced I would be accompanying him on it, I couldn't stop laughing. He said it was cheaper than a drum machine, and as I was a competent typist, there was no reason why I couldn't learn to use it. A few weeks later we played a small selection of songs at a family party, and then did our first gig. I knew just 17 numbers.' In their first three years, Jackie and her husband did over 450 gigs and became full-time professionals.

Derry, a spare-time musician who became a full-timer after losing his job as a factory manager, has built up a busy engagement list as a pianist and accordionist. His principal activities are piano bar work in pubs and hotels, private functions, and accompanying in clubs and theatres. He has played for such artists as John Hanson, Ronnie Hilton and the Roly Polys and worked in Germany. 'I enjoy the freedom,' he said. 'No-one tells me what to do. The hours may be unsocial, but I can stay in bed on Monday morning. Most of my driving is done when there is no traffic about.' His advice: 'Be sure you're good. Have funds to cover you for a couple of years until you get established. Be as versatile as possible, and try everything that comes up. Keep yourself in front of the public.'

A former carpet fitter and part-time musician, Ian became a professional guitarist at 40, and found that the hardest part of the transition was freeing his mind of the idea of 'working nine to five, and receiving x pounds every week or month.' He stressed the need to 'make sure you've put enough work into learning your craft.' Also, he advised, 'Never stop thinking of ideas that will further your career, but think them through carefully and pursue only the most realistic. Use your time to the best advantage by practising, learning, phoning and writing to contacts for work, playing with as many people as possible. Build something – a group or style – that you can sell.'

Trained musicians can also work as teachers, therapists, administrators and instrument technicians. Students over 40 are a rarity at leading training establishments such as the London College of Music and the Guildhall School of Music, but such applicants are considered on their merits.

Whatever your background, it seems you are never too old to make music or, indeed, to compose it. Andy Hamilton, a Birmingham jazz saxophonist, cut his first record at 72 and is probably the oldest man to have his disc debut on Radio One, while Buckinghamshire pensioner and composer Minna Keal had her first symphony performed live at the Proms when she was 80.

Dancing

There is little realistic chance of making a late start as a professional dance performer. By the age of 40 most 'hoofers' are thinking of hanging up their shoes if they haven't already done so. An unusual exception are the jolly, high kicking Roly Polys, who made the big-time in middle age, but all had professional dancing experience long before joining the troupe. However, if you are experienced with the taps or know your ballet steps well enough, you could run classes for youngsters, or even for the over-40s.

The somewhat less physical activity of ballroom dancing offers another possible alternative. A West Midland contributor told me how, with his wife, he began learning to dance for something to do on Sunday evenings. He was then 43. As he became more proficient he started assisting the instructor at a children's dance class, and in due course took qualifying examinations in ballroom and Latin American with the International Dance Teachers' Association (IDTA). After turning professional he ran dancing classes in a hotel, then opened his own school in a local club. His work in ballroom dancing has completely transformed his life, he said. 'There are very few pastimes or sports which can, like ballroom dancing, be shared by the whole family, including grandparents and kids.'

CHECK LIST

- Be realistic; make sure you're good at what you do before trying to turn professional.
- Remember – most work is on a freelance basis.
- If your age *does* prove prohibitive as a performer, consider teaching the subject instead.

12

Abroad Perspective

WORKING OVERSEAS

Experienced, well qualified people from the UK have long been welcomed by employers in many countries around the world, and the demand still exists today, especially in the developing economies of the Third World.

While the employment packages which over the years have lured thousands of Britons overseas may not always be quite as lucrative as they once were, many still offer attractive salaries and generous fringe benefits. A major incentive for many is the prospect of returning home with a handsome nest-egg to resume a previous career, embark on a new one, or live in comfortable retirement. The downside is that the cost of living in some of the host countries can be high, the climate and living conditions disagreeable, and the posts isolated with few amenities and little social life. Family harmony can be severely tested by an alien culture and environment and language difficulties.

Government agencies

A considerable proportion of expatriates find their overseas jobs through the Overseas Development Administration or the Crown Agents, who recruit for overseas governments and agencies and engage staff to work on British aid programmes in other countries.

Some recruits are paid directly by one of the UK agencies to work, for example, on technical cooperative schemes in developing countries, while others are paid by the host government or organisation concerned. UK equivalent salaries are normally augmented to cover the additional cost of living overseas and expenditure on such items as special clothing. Passages to and from the country concerned are usually paid, as are holiday visits to the overseas location by children left to continue their schooling in Britain. Allowances may also be given to cover medical treatment, children's education and accommodation.

The ODA said that most of the people they employ for assignments overseas have specific professional and technical qualifications and a good deal of experience in their particular fields. Some are 'career expatriates for whom a mid-life change would be to settle down quietly in the Home Counties' while for others it is their first experience of working overseas.

Angus, a 46-year-old director of nursing services with special expertise in the field of mental handicap, gave up his post in Lancashire to work as a manpower adviser on a health project in southern Tanzania. His brief was to provide expert help in such areas as management of hospitals, identifying training needs of indigenous personnel and the provision of training either locally or overseas. The main satisfactions of the job, said Angus, were helping the Tanzanians in their fight against poverty and disease, the opportunity to influence thinking and give direction to new ideas and developments, being at 'grass roots' level again, and rediscovering his own strengths and weaknesses. Separation from his children (at boarding school in the UK) was difficult, but giving up 'western' habits had been a blessing and the uncertainty about what the future held had an element of excitement. His advice to other would-be expatriates: 'Don't rush in. Prepare meticulously. Hesitate if you are career orientated. Have your future potential alternatives clear in your mind. Be clear about your motives. Be sure your family are really supportive. Be healthy.'

A former chief executive with a district council in the south of England, Robin was 52 when he was appointed to a similar level position in Malawi. He had to tackle serious problems, including inefficiency, organisational disarray, and shortage of management staff, but was able to find satisfaction in effecting permanent improvements to urban government. 'Get a thorough briefing on the local situation before going abroad, and ascertain why an expatriate is needed,' he advised. 'Be absolutely clear about the fringe benefits and take professional advice on tax matters. Overseas service offers new and lucrative careers to professionals over 50, who are much in demand because of their experience and lesser incidence of domestic ties and responsibilities, but you need to be resilient and prepared to accept local administrators on their own terms.'

A former tax inspector and staff trainer with the Inland Revenue, Robert spent three years with the tax department of the Ministry of Finance in Mauritius. He told me, 'My work involved devising, setting up and running a training course for tax inspectors, and advising the Government of Mauritius on tax matters generally and specifically on methods to counter the widespread tax evasion. There was huge scope for using imagination, initiative and ingenuity. It is satisfying to discover at over 50 that one is capable of producing better work than ever before.'

British Council

Many mature men and women find overseas posts in the education and training field through the British Council. Teachers, especially English language specialists, and technician trainers have been in particular demand.

The Council also offers career opportunities on its staff to well qualified people up to the age of 50 to help in its work of promoting Britain abroad and fostering cultural, educational and technical cooperation with other countries. Good health is essential and a knowledge of or aptitude for learning languages is a considerable plus factor.

Commonwealth recruitment

Experts and advisers to meet specific requests from developing countries are recruited by the Commonwealth Fund for Technical Co-operation (CFTC), the technical assistance arm of the Commonwealth Secretariat. Recruitment is also undertaken by the London offices of some overseas governments, such as Ghana, Malawi, Nigeria, Zambia and Sierra Leone.

United Nations

Qualified Britons are recruited by the United Nations and its agencies, such as the World Health Organisation (WHO), the International Monetary Fund (IMF), the Organisation for Economic Co-operation and Development (OECD), and the UN Educational, Scientific and Cultural Organisation (UNESCO). Most of the jobs are professional, administrative or secretarial.

Robert, a former director of education with a midlands local authority, and his wife, Jill, who was a project director with a national educational body, teamed up to work as regional educational planners in Grenada and Barbados. Employed under the auspices of UNESCO, their brief was to help ministries of education, particularly in small territories, to develop a capacity for long-term planning and produce educational policy plans. They enjoyed being able to work and travel together, learning how to relate and be effective in a new culture, and earning the trust and respect of local colleagues. They found the work progressively rewarding, but faced such problems as having too little time within the contract brief, difficult communications within the region, the multi-varied political, bureaucratic and administrative structures, coping with the climate while working, and missing family and friends. 'The Caribbean sounds and is attractive, but residing and working there is quite different from being a tourist,' said Robert. His advice: 'Be prepared to learn and be humble; have strong leisure interests outside work; mix with the locals and not just expatriates; don't expect a standard of living and access to the kind of material goods and services to which you have been accustomed; and take care of yourself because health services are not extensive.'

Check list
- Be clear about your motives.
- Thoroughly research conditions in the host country before accepting an offer of employment.
- Accept the locals on their own terms and mix with them.

Diplomatic service
The Foreign and Commonwealth Office is prepared to consider applications for administrative grade posts in the Diplomatic Service from high calibre men and women up to the age of 52 and, for exceptional candidates, even beyond that. Entry levels may be at grade 7 or 8 for those with good degrees or grade 9 (equivalent to an executive officer in the Home Civil Service).

Competitions for the posts are well advertised in the national press and elsewhere.

European Community
The arrival of the single market at the end of 1992 removed trade barriers and allowed free movement of people, capital, goods and services. Subject to certain provisos, each member state recognises professional qualifications awarded by the others. Although some limitations remain, for example with regard to public services, all working people effectively enjoy the same rights of employment as indigenous workers.

To seek employment in another EC country, contact the Overseas Placing Unit through your local Jobcentre. There is an exchange of information on job vacancies between member countries within the Community. Private employment agencies also handle vacancies, and many positions are advertised in the national newspapers and specialist publications.

Booklets on the EC helpful to job seekers are issued by the Department of Trade and Industry and the Employment Department. Career opportunities for well qualified administrators, linguists, professional and scientific staff sometimes occur at the European Commission and other EC bodies.

VOLUNTARY WORK

There is a continuing need for volunteers with trade or professional skills to serve abroad for a minimum of one year under the auspices of the four constituent organisations of the British Voluntary Programme — the Catholic Institute for International Relations, International Voluntary Service, United Nations Association International Service, and Voluntary Services Overseas (VSO). Volunteers normally receive board, lodging and pocket money. Travel costs etc. are paid by the sending organisation.

An independent group which places many older people in short-term appointments abroad is the British Executive Service Overseas (BESO). Demand for the experience and skills of BESO volunteers have been increasing around the world. They have been called on to handle such assignments as hotel staff training in Dominica, port problems in Ethiopia, brewing in China, bee-keeping in Vietnam and shoe manufacturing in Cyprus. The airfare and an allowance for the volunteer and spouse are met by BESO and the beneficiary in the host country meets the cost of local accommodation and transport and provides a small subsistence allowance for the volunteer. Most of the placements are financed by the ODA.

Some religious denominations sponsor missionary organisations, which send teachers, agriculturalists, engineers, medical workers, secretaries and other skilled people to a number of overseas countries. You have to undergo training, and are expected to be a committed Christian. Further information can be obtained from the Conference for World Missions, British Council of Churches, or from individual missionary societies such as the Church Missionary Society and the Religious Society of Friends (Quakers).

EMIGRATION

Though career ambitions may be a motivating factor for many over-40s who decide to emigrate, it is not usually the only one. Other considerations can include a more agreeable lifestyle, a better place to bring up the children, a sunnier climate, and a kinder tax system.

Entry regulations vary from country to country, but the

conditions imposed by Australia, New Zealand and Canada —
traditionally popular destinations for Britons — have become more
stringent in recent years. Each country sets yearly quotas and, apart
from those accepted as close relatives of existing residents or on
humanitarian grounds, most immigrants are selected on the basis of
their skills and the contribution they can make to the host economy.
Points systems are used which take account of such factors as
occupation, work experience, education, sponsoring relatives in the
destination country, knowledge of English (also French in Canada),
funds and age.

You may have to satisfy the immigration authorities concerned
that you have a job awaiting you for which a suitably qualified
resident cannot be found, or that you have a viable business plan
and the resources to start an enterprise which is likely to offer
employment to local people. If you are sponsored by a close relative
he or she has to guarantee that you will not become a burden to the
taxpayers.

While the Canadians and Australians may accept you up to
normal UK retirement age providing you fulfil other immigration
requirements, the New Zealanders set an upper age limit of 55. It
may, however, be possible to live in retirement in one of the popular
migrant countries if you can satisfy your hosts that you have
sufficient funds to sustain you for the foreseeable future. Whatever
your age you will need to be in reasonably good health and not have
a criminal record. You will be liable to a processing charge for the
handling of your immigration application, which can run into
several hundred pounds. Entry regulations change from time to
time, so to obtain up-to-date information you should contact the
UK migration offices of the country in which you are interested. A
valuable source of current information on employment, the cost of
houses, cars and other items in your chosen country are its
newspapers. The appropriate migration authorities will advise
how to obtain sample copies.

The evidence suggests that most immigrants adapt successfully to
their new lives; some don't settle happily but make the best of it and
stay put; and a small minority pack their bags and head for home.
Contributions from many parts of Australia, New Zealand and
Canada, and my own experience as an emigrant in Canada, suggest
that becoming successfully assimilated can be as much about
attitude as about occupation or personal circumstances.

Here is a selection of comments received from men and women
who emigrated after 40:

Leaving wasn't without trauma and wondering if we had done the right thing.

I feel that emigrating at our age helped us to settle more easily. Not having many working years ahead of us, we knew that if we didn't make a go of it, we would have ended up back in the UK worse off than when we left.

Anyone contemplating emigration to Australia should come and visit the place before burning their bridges. It's cheaper than selling up and starting again if you don't like it.

I have been back to England three times, but I couldn't live there now. It's too cold, and I've got used to the warm sunshine and casual lifestyle here in Western Australia.

Australia may not be perfect, and like most countries has its problems, but it is a fairer country than Britain.

The choice was between Australia and New Zealand because of their climate (Canada was ruled out for this reason), stable political systems and British traditions. We chose New Zealand in preference to Australia because it seemed a gentler country.

New Zealand is a beautiful uncrowded place. In my view the quality of life is higher than in Britain, partly due to such things as an unpolluted atmosphere, wide open spaces, lack of crowds, milder climate, excellent sporting facilities, the beauty of the countryside which is mainly untouched and unspoiled, and the friendliness of almost everyone you meet.

We have found New Zealand towns small and easy to live in; a good place to bring up children.

I am happily settled myself, but have met immigrants who find New Zealand life provincial and boring.

Canada is not predominantly British any more. In recent years immigrants and refugees have come in large numbers from all over the world. It has become much more cosmopolitan.

The long winter here in Ontario is a bit trying, but the dry cold suits me better than Britain's damp days.

Canadian education is very good indeed. Children from families of almost any level of income have the chance to go to university, given the desire, the will and the ability.

Our belief that Canada held out good prospects has been wonderfully borne out. There is lots of room, lots of scope and opportunity for anyone willing to take advantage of what is available and work for it.

CHECK LIST

- Try to visit your chosen country before going to settle.
- Arrange work and accommodation in advance.
- Take sufficient capital to help you get established.

Last Word

'We did it, and so can you!' That is the fundamental message from contributors to this book for all those over 40 who may be contemplating a change of career. The evidence suggests that, even in a time of high unemployment, the range of opportunities for mature career changers is far wider than often supposed. And a variety of factors are working in their favour — demographic trends showing a reduction in the number of school leavers and the rate of growth of the working population, an unprecedented range of educational and training opportunities, plenty of help and encouragement for new businesses, an increasingly influential lobby against ageism, and signs that a growing number of employers are recognising, if only through enlightened self-interest, the principle that if you are good enough to do a job, you are young enough.

Could this be your moment to 'go for it'? Whatever your decision, **Good Luck**!

Useful Addresses

ABROAD, WORKING

British Council, 10 Spring Gardens, London SW1A 2BN. Tel. 071 930 8466.

British Executive Service Overseas, 164 Vauxhall Bridge Road, London SW1V 2RB. Tel. 071 630 0644.

Catholic Institute for International Relations, 22 Coleman Fields, London N1 7AF. Tel. 071 354 0883.

Church Missionary Society, Partnership House, 157 Waterloo Road, London SE1 8UU. Tel. 071 928 8681.

Commonwealth Fund for Technical Co-operation, Commonwealth Secretariat, Marlborough House, Pall Mall, London SW1Y 5HX. Tel. 071 839 3411.

Crown Agents, TR Division, St Nicholas House, St Nicholas Road, Sutton, Surrey SM1 1EL. Tel. 081 643 3311.

DSS Overseas Branch, Benton Point Road, Newcastle upon Tyne NE98 1YX. Tel. 0632 857111.

Inland Revenue, Claims Branch, Foreign Division, Merton Road, Bootle L69 9BL. Tel. 051 922 6363.

Overseas Development Administration (ODA), Abercrombie House, Eaglesham Road, East Kilbride G75 8EA. Tel. 035 52 41199.

United Nations Association International Service (UNIS), 3 Whitehall Court, London SW1A 2EL. Tel. 071 930 0679.

Voluntary Service Overseas (VSO), 9 Belgrave Square, London SW1X 8PW. Tel. 071 235 5191.

ACCOUNTANCY

Association of Accountancy Technicians, 21 Jockey's Fields, London WC1R 4BN. Tel. 071 837 8600.

Chartered Association of Certified Accountants, 29 Lincoln's Inn Fields, London WC2A 3EE. Tel. 071 242 6855.

Institute of Chartered Accountants in England and Wales, Chartered Accountants' Hall, PO Box 433, Moorgate Place, London EC2P 2BJ. Tel. 071 628 7060; **ICA of Scotland,** 27

Queen Street, Edinburgh EH2 1LA. Tel. 031 325 5673.

ACTING

British Actors Equity Association, 8 Harley Street, London W1N 2AB. Tel. 071 636 6367.
National Council for Drama Training, 5 Tavistock Place, London WC1H 9SS. Tel. 071 387 3650.
Royal Scottish Academy of Music and Drama, 100 Renfrew Street, Glasgow G2 3DB. Tel. 041 332 4101.

ACUPUNCTURE

British Acupuncture Association and Register, 34 Alderney Street, London SW1V 4EU. Tel. 071 834 1012.
British College of Acupuncture, 8 Hunter Street, London WC1N. Tel. 071 833 8164.
College of Traditional Chinese Acupuncture, Tao House, Queensway, Leamington Spa, Warwickshire. Tel. 0926 422121.
London School of Acupuncture and Traditional Chinese Medicine, 36 Featherstone Street, London EC1Y 8QX. Tel. 071 490 0513.

ADVERTISING

Advertising Association, Abford House, 15 Wilton Rd, London SW1V 1NJ. Tel. 071 828 4831.
Communication, Advertising and Marketing Education Foundation (CAM), Abford House, 15 Wilton Rd, London SW1V 1NJ. Tel. 071 828 7506.

AGRICULTURE

Careers Education and Training Information Centre, Royal Agricultural Society of England, National Agricultural Centre, Kenilworth, Warwickshire CV8 2LZ. Tel. 0203 696969.
Ministry of Agriculture, Fisheries and Food/Agricultural Development and Advisory Service (ADAS), Nobel House, 17 Smith Square, London SW1P 3JR. Tel. 071 238 5641 or MAFF divisional offices.

AMBULANCE SERVICE

Ambulance Service Institute, Kingsway Hospital, Kingsway, Derby. Tel. 0332 372441.

ANIMALS

Animal Care College (Canine Studies Institute), London Road, Bracknell, Berkshire RG12 6QN. Tel. 0344 420898)

British Horse Society, British Equestrian Centre, Stoneleigh, Kenilworth, Warwickshire CV8 2LR. Tel. 0203 696697.

British Veterinary Nursing Association, The Seedbed Centre, Coldharbour Road, Harlow, Essex CM19 5AF. Tel. 0279 45067.

College of Animal Welfare, Wood Green Animal Shelters, King's Bush Farm, London Road, Huntingdon, Cambridgeshire PE18 8LJ. Tel. 0480 831177.

Guide Dogs for the Blind Association, Hillfields, Burghfield Common, Reading RG7 3YG. Tel. 0734 835555.

Kennel Club, 1 Clarges Street, Piccadilly, London W1Y 8AB. Tel. 071 493 6651.

PDSA, Whitechapel Way, Priorslee, Telford, Shropshire TF2 9PQ. Tel. 0952 290999.

Royal College of Veterinary Surgeons, 32 Belgrave Square, London SW1X 8QP. Tel. 071 235 4971/2.

RSPCA, Causeway, Horsham, West Sussex RH12 1HG. Tel. 0403 64181.

University Federation for Animal Welfare, 8 Hamilton Close, South Mimms, Potters Bar, Hertfordshire EN6 3QD. Tel. 0707 58202.

ANTIQUES

British Antique Dealers Association Ltd., 20 Rutland Gate, London SW7 1BD. Tel. 071 589 4128.

London and Provincial Antique Dealers Association, 3 Cheval Place, London SW7. Tel. 071 584 7911.

ARCHAEOLOGY

Archaeology Abroad, 31-34 Gordon Square, London WC1H 0PY.

Council for British Archaeology, 112 Kennington Road, London SE11 6RE. Tel. 071 582 0494.

ARCHITECTURE

Architects Registration Council of the UK, 73 Hallam Street, London W1N 6EE. Tel. 071 580 5861.

Royal Institute of British Architects, 66 Portland Place, London W1N 4AD. Tel. 071 580 5533.

ARCHIVIST

Society of Archivists, Information House, 20-24 Old Street, London EC1V 9AP. Tel. 071 253 4488.

AUDIOLOGY

British Society of Audiology, 80 Brighton Road, Reading RG6 1PS. Tel. 0754 660622.

BAKERY

National Council for Baking Education, 20 Bedford Square, London WC1B 3HF. Tel. 071 580 4252.

BEAUTY THERAPY

International Health and Beauty Therapy Training Board, PO Box 21, Bognor Regis, West Sussex PO22 7PS. Tel. 0243 860339.
International Therapy Examination Council, James House, Oakelbrook Mill, Newent, Gloucestershire GL18 1HD. Tel. 0531 821875.

BOAT SERVICES

Association of Pleasure Craft Operators, 35a High Street, Newport, Shropshire TF10 8JW. Tel. 0952 813572.

BOOKSELLER

Booksellers Association of Great Britain and Ireland, 272 Vauxhall Bridge Road, London SW1V 1BA. Tel. 071 834 5477.

BUILDING INDUSTRY

Construction Industry Training Board, Bircham Newton Training Centre, near Kings Lynn, Norfolk PE31 6RH. Tel. 0553 776677.

BUSINESS

Department of Employment, Caxton House, Tothill Street, London SW1H 9NF. Tel. 071 273 3000.
Department of Trade and Industry, Ashdown House, 123 Victoria Street, London SW1E 6RB, general enquiries – tel. 071 215 5000; enterprise initiative helpline – freephone 0800 500 200 or contact a regional DTI office.

Federation of Small Businesses, 32 St Anne's Road West, Lytham St Annes, Lancashire FY8 1NY. Tel. 0253 720911.

Rural Development Commission, 11 Cowley Street, London SW1P 3NA. Tel. 071 276 6969.

BUTCHER

Institute of Meat, Langford, Bristol BS18 7DY. Tel. 0934 853018.

BUTLER

Ivor Spencer International School for Butler Administrators/ Personal Assistants, 12 Little Bornes, Alleyn Park, London SE21 8SE. Tel. 081 670 5585.

CAREERS

Guidance: **Career Analysts,** Career House, 90 Gloucester Place, London W1H 4BL. Tel. 071 935 5452.

Information:

Careers and Occupational Information Centre, Moorfoot, Sheffield S1 4PQ. Tel 0742 753275.

Central Services Unit, Association of Graduate Careers Advisory Services (AGCAS), Armstrong House, Oxford Road, Manchester M1 7ED. Tel. 061 236 9763.

Training loans: Freepost, Career Development, PO Box 99, Sudbury, Suffolk CO10 6BR (information on Department of Employment career development loans).

CAREERS ADVISER

Institute of Careers Guidance, 27a Lower High Street, Stourbridge, West Midlands DY8 1TA. Tel. 0384 376464.

Kent College for the Careers Service, College Road, Hextable, Swanley, Kent BR8 7RN. Tel. 0322 64407/8.

CATERING

(see *Hotels and Catering*)

CHARITIES

Institute of Charity Fundraising Managers, Market Towers, 1 Nine Elms Lane, London SW8 5NQ. Tel. 071 627 3436.

CHILDMINDING

National Childminders Association, 8 Masons Hill, Bromley, Kent BR2 9EY. Tel. 081 464 6164.

CHIROPODY

Institute of Chiropodists, 91 Lord Street, Southport PR8 1SA. Tel. 0704 46141.
Society of Chiropodists, 53 Welbeck Street, London W1M 7HE. Tel. 071 486 3381.

CHIROPRACTIC

Anglo-European College of Chiropractic, Parkwood Road, Bournemouth, Dorset. Tel. 0202 431021.
British Chiropractic Association, Premier House, 10 Greycoat Place, London SW1P 1SB. Tel. 071 222 8866.

CIVIL SERVICE

Recruitment and Assessment Services Agency, Alencon Link, Basingstoke, Hampshire RG21 1JB. Tel. 0256 29222.

CLOTHES SHOP

Clothing and Allied Industries Training Board, 80 Richardshaw Lane, Pudsey, Leeds LS28 6AA. Tel. 0532 393355.

COASTGUARD

HM Coastguard Headquarters, Department of Transport, Sunley House, 90 High Holborn, London WC1V 6LP. Tel. 071 405 6911.

COMPANY SECRETARY

Institute of Chartered Secretaries and Administrators, Careers Department, 16 Park Crescent, London W1N 4AH. Tel. 071 580 4741.

COMPLEMENTARY MEDICINE

Institute of Complementary Medicine, 21 Portland Place, London W1N 3AF. Tel. 071 636 9543.

COMPUTERS

British Computer Society, 13 Mansfield Street, London W1M 0BP. Tel. 071 637 0471.

CONFECTIONER, TOBACCONIST, NEWSAGENT(CTN)

National Federation of Retail Newsagents, 11 Sekforde Street, London EC1R 0HD. Tel. 071 253 4225.
Retail Confectioners and Tobacconists Association, 53 Christchurch Avenue, London N12 0DH. Tel. 081 445 6344.

COUNTRYSIDE

Conservation: **Royal Society for Nature Conservation,** The Green, Nettleham, Lincolnshire LN2 2NR. Tel. 0522 544400.

COUNSELLING

British Association for Counselling, 37a Sheep Street, Rugby, Warwickshire CV21 3BX. Tel. 0788 78328/9
Relate, Herbert Gray College, Little Church Street, Rugby, Warwickshire CV21 3AP. Tel. 0788 573241.

CRAFTS

Crafts Council, 12 Waterloo Place, London SW1Y 4AU. Tel. 071 930 4811.
West Dean College, West Dean, Chichester, West Sussex PO18 0QZ. Tel. 01243 63 301.

CREATIVE WRITING

Society of Authors, 84 Drayton Gardens, London SW10 9SB. Tel. 071 373 6642.
Writers' Guild of Great Britain, 430 Edgware Road, London W2 1EH. Tel. 071 723 8074.
Arvon Foundation, Totleigh Barton, Sheepwash, Devon EX21 5NS. Tel. 040 923 338; Lumb Bank, Hebden Bridge, West Yorkshire HX7 6DF. Tel. 0422 843714; Moniack Mhor, Moniack, Kirkhill, Inverness IV5 7PQ. Tel. 0463 833336.
Writers' Summer School: Philippa Boland, The Red House, Mardens Hill, Crowborough, East Sussex TN6 1XN. Tel. 0892 653943.
Writers' Holidays: Anne Hobbs, 30 Pant Road, Newport, Gwent

NP9 5PR. Tel. 0633 854976.

CUSTOMS AND EXCISE OFFICER

HM Customs and Excise, New King's Beam House, 22 Upper Ground, London SE1 9PJ. Tel. 071 620 1313.

DANCING

Imperial Society of Teachers of Dancing, Euston Hall, Birkenhead Street, London WC1H 8BE. Tel. 071 837 9967.

DENTISTRY

General Dental Council, 37 Wimpole Street, London W1M 8DQ. Tel. 071 486 2171.

National Examining Board for Dental Surgery Assistants, DSA House, 29 London Street, Fleetwood, Lancashire FY7 6JY. Tel. 03917 78631.

DESIGN

Chartered Society of Designers, 29 Bedford Square, London WC1B 3EG. Tel. 071 631 1510.

Design Council, 28 Haymarket, London SW1Y 4SU. Tel. 071 839 8000; Scotland 041 221 6121; Northern Ireland 0232 238452.

DIETETICS

British Dietetics Association, Elizabeth House, 22 Suffolk Street, Queensway, Birmingham B1 1LS. Tel. 021 643 5483.

DRIVING EXAMINER

Department of Transport, 2 Marsham Street, London SW1P 3EB. Tel. 071 276 0888.

DRIVING INSTRUCTOR

Department of Transport, 2 Marsham Street, London SW1P 3EB. Tel. 071 276 3000.

Driving Standards Agency, Stanley House, Talbot Street, Nottingham NG1 5GU. Tel. 0602 474222.

Driving Instructors Association, Lion Green Road, Coulsdon, Surrey CR3 2NL. Tel. 081 660 3333.

EDUCATION

Department of Education, Sanctuary Buildings, Great Smith Street, London SW1 3BT. Tel. 071 925 5000.

Open University, Central Enquiry Service, PO Box 71, Milton Keynes MK7 6AA. Tel. 0908 274066; Scotland 031 225 2889.

Polytechnics Central Admissions System (PCAS), PO Box 67, Cheltenham, Gloucestershire GL50 3AP. Tel. 0242 227788.

Universities Central Council on Admissions (UCCA), PO Box 28, Cheltenham, Gloucestershire GL52 3SF. Tel. 0242 222444.

Workers Educational Association, Temple House, 9 Upper Berkeley Street, London W1H 8BY. Tel. 071 402 5608.

Examination organisations

Business and Technology Education Council (BTEC), Central House, Upper Woburn Place, London WC1H 0HH. Tel. 071 388 3288.

City and Guilds of London Institute, 46 Britannia Street, London WC1X 9RG. Tel. 071 278 2468.

London Chamber of Commerce and Industry Examinations Board, Marlowe House, Sidcup, Kent DA15 7BJ. Tel. 081 302 0261.

Royal Society of Arts Examinations Board, Westwood Way, Coventry CV4 8HS. Tel. 0203 470033.

Vocational training

National Council for Vocational Qualifications, 222 Euston Road, London W1 2BZ. Tel. 071 387 9898.

Scottish Vocational Education Council (SCOT-VEC), Hanover House, 24 Douglas Street, Glasgow G2 7NQ. Tel. 041 248 7900.

Correspondence colleges

Council for Accreditation of Correspondence Colleges, 27 Marylebone Road, London NW1 5JS. Tel. 071 935 5391.

National Extension College (NEC), 18 Brooklands Avenue, Cambridge CB2 2HN. Tel. 0223 316644.

EMIGRATION

Migration Branch, Australian High Commission, Australia

House, Strand, London WC2B 4LA. Tel. 071 379 4334.
Canadian High Commission, Immigration Section, MacDonald House, 38 Grosvenor Street, London W1X 0AA. Tel. 071 409 2071.
New Zealand Immigration Service, 3rd Floor, New Zealand House, 80 Haymarket, London SW1Y 4TQ. Tel. 071 973 0366.

EMPLOYMENT AGENCIES

Employment Agency Licensing Office, 2 Church Road, Stanmore, Middlesex. Tel. 081 954 7677.
Institute of Employment Consultants, 6 Guildford Road, Woking, Surrey GU22 7PX. Tel. 0483 766442.

ENGINEERING

Engineering Careers Information Service, 54 Clarendon Street, Watford WD1 1LB. Tel. *freephone* 0800 282167; Glasgow Tel. 041 332 9393.

ENVIRONMENTAL HEALTH OFFICER

Institution of Environment Health Officers, Chadwick House, Rushworth Street, London SE1 0QT. Tel. 071 928 6006.

ESTATE AGENCY

College of Estate Management, Whiteknights, Reading RG6 2AW. Tel. 0734 861101.
Incorporated Society of Valuers and Auctioneers, 3 Cadogan Gate, London SW1X 0AS. Tel. 071 235 2282.

EXPORT

British Overseas Trade Board, Kingsgate House, 66-77 Victoria Street, London SW1H 0ET. Tel. 071 276 3000.
Institute of Export, 64 Clifton Street, London EC2 4HB. Tel. 071 247 9812.
Institute of Freight Forwarders, Redfern House, Browells Lane, Feltham, Middlesex TW13 7EP. Tel. 081 844 2266.

FARRIERY

Farriery Training Service, PO Box 49, East of England Showground, Peterborough, Cambridgeshire PE2 0GU. Tel. 0733 234451.

FILMS AND TELEVISION

British Film Institute, 21 Stephen Street, London W1P 1PL. Tel. 071 255 1444.

London International Film School, 24 Shelton Street, London WC2H 9HP. Tel. 071 836 9642.

National Film and Television School, Station Road, Beaconsfield, Buckinghamshire. Tel. 0494 671234.

FINANCIAL ADVISER

FIMBRA (Financial Intermediaries, Managers and Brokers Association), Hertsmere House, Hertsmere Road, London E14. Tel. 071 538 8860.

LAUTRO (Life Assurance and Unit Trust Regulatory Organisation Ltd.), Centre Point, 103 New Oxford Street, London WC1A 1DD. Tel. 071 379 0444.

FORESTRY

Arboriculture Association, Ampfield House, Ampfield, Nr Romsey, Hampshire SO51 9PA. Tel. 0794 68717.

British Christmas Tree Growers Association, Secretary, 12 Lauriston Road, London SW19 4TQ. Tel. 081 946 2695.

Forestry Training Council, 231 Corstorphine Road, Edinburgh EH12 7AT. Tel. 031 334 0303.

FOSTERING

National Foster Care Association, Francis House, Francis Street, London SW1P 1DE. Tel. 071 828 6266.

FRANCHISES

British Franchise Association, Franchise Chambers, Thames View, Newtown Road, Henley on Thames, Oxfordshire RG9 1HG. Tel. 0491 578050.

FUNERAL WORK

National Association of Funeral Directors, 618 Warwick Road, Solihull, West Midlands B91 1AA. Tel. 021 711 1343.

GENEALOGY

Association of Genealogists and Record Agents, 29 Badgers

Close, Horsham, West Sussex RH12 5RU.
Society of Genealogists, 14 Charterhouse Buildings, Goswell Road, London EC1M 7BA. Tel. 071 251 8799.

GRAPHOLOGY

International Graphoanalysis Society, Stonedge, Dunkerton, Bath BA2 8AS. Tel. 0761 427809.

HAIRDRESSING

Hairdressing Training Board, 17 Silver House, Silver Street, Doncaster DN1 1HL. Tel. 0302 342837.

HEALTH SERVICE MANAGEMENT

Health Service Careers, PO Box 9B, East Molesey, Surrey KT8 0PE.
Institute of Health Services Management, Education Department, 75 Portland Place, London W1N 4AN. Tel. 071 580 5041.
NHS Training Authority, St Bartholomews Court, 18 Christmas Street, Bristol BS1 5BT. Tel. 0272 291029.

HELPING HAND SERVICES

Universal Aunts Ltd, PO Box 304, London SW4 0NN. Tel. 071 738 8937.
Homesitters Ltd., Buckland Wharf, Buckland, Aylesbury, Buckinghamshire HP22 5LQ. Tel. 0296 630730.
Motivity, 34 Percy Road, Hampton, Middlesex. Tel. 081 976 6277/5364.

HERBAL MEDICINE

National Institute of Medical Herbalists, 9 Palace Gate, Exeter, Devon EX1 1JA. Tel. 0392 426022.
School of Herbal Medicine and Phytotherapy, 148 Forest Road, Tunbridge Wells, Kent. Tel. 0892 30400.
School of Herbal Medicine, Bucksteep Manor, Bodle Street Green, Hailsham, Sussex. Tel. 0323 833812.

HOME ECONOMIST

Institute of Home Economics Ltd., Aldwych House, 71-91 Aldwych, London WC2B 4HN. Tel. 071 404 5532.

HOMEOPATHY

British Homeopathy Association, 27a Devonshire Street, London W1N 1RJ. Tel. 071 935 2163.

HORTICULTURE

Horticultural Education Association: Careers Secretary, Askham Bryan College of Agriculture & Horticulture, Askham Bryan, York YO2 3PR. Tel. 0904 702121.

Royal Botanic Gardens, Kew, Richmond, Surrey TW9 3AB. Tel. 081 940 1171.

Royal Botanic Gardens, Edinburgh EH3 5LR. Tel. 031 552 7171.

Royal Horticultural Society, 80 Vincent Square, London SW1P 2PE. Tel. 071 834 4333; the Institute of Horticulture is at the same address.

HOTELS AND CATERING

Hotel, Catering and Institutional Management Association, 191 Trinity Road, London SW17 7HN. Tel. 081 672 4251, and Capital House, 9 Logie Mill, Edinburgh EH7 4HG. Tel. 031 337 0464.

Hotel and Catering Training Company, International House, High Street, London W5 5DB. Tel. 081 579 2400.

HYPNOTHERAPY

British Hypnotherapy Association, 1 Wythburn Place, London W1H 5WL. Tel. 071 723 4443.

National College of Hypnosis and Psychotherapy, 12 Cross Street, Nelson, Lancashire BB9 7EN. Tel. 0282 699378.

INSURANCE

British Insurance and Investment Association, 14 Bevis Marks, London EC3A 7NT. Tel. 071 623 9043.

Chartered Insurance Institute, 20 Aldermanbury, London EC2V 7HY. Tel. 071 606 3835.

Insurance Brokers Registration Council, 15 St Helens Place, London EC3A 6DS. Tel. 071 588 4387.

INTERPRETER

(see *Translator*)

INTRODUCTION AGENCIES

Association of British Introduction Agencies, 25 Abingdon Road, London W8 6AH. Tel. 071 937 2800.
Society of Marriage Bureaux, 1 Mandeville Place, London W1M 5LB. Tel. 071 935 6408.

JEWELLER

Gemmological Association, 27 Greville Street, London EC1N 8SU. Tel. 071 404 3334.
National Association of Goldsmiths, 78 Luke Street, London EC2A 4PY. Tel. 071 613 4445.

JOURNALISM

Pre-entry Training Course in Journalism: Manager, Cornwall College, Pool, Redruth, Cornwall TR15 3RD. Tel. 0209 712911.
National Council for the Training of Journalists, Carlton House, Hemnall Street, Epping, Essex CM16. Tel. 0378 72395.
Periodicals Training Council, Imperial House, 15 Kingsway, London WC2. Tel. 071 836 8798.
National Union of Journalists, Acorn House, 314 Gray's Inn Road, London WC1X 8DP. Tel. 072 278 7916.

LAW

Barristers/advocates:
England and Wales — The student officer at one of the Inns of Court: **Inner Temple,** London EC4Y 7HL; **Middle Temple,** London EC4Y 9AT; **Lincoln's Inn,** London WC2A 3TL, and **Gray's Inn,** London WC1R 5EU; the **Council of Legal Education,** Inns of Court School of Law, 4 Gray's Inn Place, London WC1R 5DX. Tel. 071 405 5907.
Scotland — The Clerk, Faculty of Advocates, Advocates' Library, Parliament House, Edinburgh EH1 1RF. Tel. 031 226 5071.
Northern Ireland — The Honorable Society of the Inn of Court of Northern Ireland, Royal Courts of Justice, Belfast BT1 3JF. Tel. 0232 235111 ext. 2201.

Legal executives:
Institute of Legal Executives, Kempston Manor, Kempston, Bedford MK42 7AB. Tel. 02334 841000.
Licenced conveyancers:
Council for Licenced Conveyancers, Golden Cross House,

Duncannon Street, London WC2N 4JF. Tel. 071 210 4560.
Solicitors:
Careers and Recruitment Service, Law Society, 227/8 Strand, London WC2R 1BA. Tel. 071 242 1222.
Law Society of Scotland, 26 Drumsheugh Gardens, Edinburgh EH3 7YR. Tel. 031 226 7411.
Law Society of Northern Ireland, Law Society House, 90-106 Victoria Street, Belfast BT1 3JZ. Tel. 0232 231614/5.

LEISURE MANAGEMENT

Institute of Leisure and Amenity Management, Education and Training Unit, ILAM House, Lower Basildon, Reading, Berkshire. RG8 9NE. Tel. 0491 873558.
Institute of Baths and Recreation Management, Gifford House, 36-38 Sherrard Street, Melton Mowbray, Leicestershire LE13 1XJ. Tel. 0664 65531.

LIBRARIAN

Education Department, Library Association, 7 Ridgmount Street, London WC1E 7AE. Tel. 071 636 7543.

LOCAL GOVERNMENT

Local Government Training Board, Arndale House, The Arndale Centre, Luton LU1 2TS. Tel. 0582 451166.

MANAGEMENT

British Institute of Management, Management House, Cottingham Road, Corby, Northamptonshire NN17 1TT. Tel. 0536 204222.
Consultancy: **The Institute of Management Consultants,** 32-33 Hatton Gardens, London EC1N 8DL. Tel. 071 242 2140.
Work study: **Institute of Management Studies,** 1 Cecil Court, London Road, Enfield, Middlesex EN2 6DD. Tel. 081 363 7452.

MARKET RESEARCH

Office of Population Censuses and Surveys, Social Surveys Division, St Catherine's House, 10 Kingsway, London WC2B 6JP. Tel. 071 242 0262.
Market Research Society, 15 Northburgh Street, London EC1V OAH. Tel. 071 490 4911.

MARKETING AND SALES

Chartered Institute of Marketing, Moor Hall, Cookham, Maidenhead, Berkshire SL6 9QH. Tel. 06285 24922.

Institute of Marketing and Sales Management, National Westminster House, 31 Upper George Street, Luton, Bedfordshire LU1 2RD. Tel. 0582 411130.

MASSAGE

Clare Maxwell-Hudson School, 87 Dartmouth Road, London NW2 4ER. Tel. 071 450 6494.

(see also *Beauty Therapy*)

MEDICINE

British Medical Association, BMA House, Tavistock Square, London WC1H 9JP. Tel. 071 387 4499.

Association of Medical Secretaries, Practice Administrators and Receptionists, Tavistock House North, Tavistock Square, London WC1H 9LN. Tel. 071 387 6005.

MUSEUMS

Museums Association, 42 Clerkenwell Close, London EC1R 0PA. Tel. 071 404 4767.

Museum Training Institute, Kershaw House, 55 Wells Street, Bradford BD1 5PS. Tel. 0274 291056.

MUSIC

Incorporated Society of Musicians, 10 Stratford Place, London W1N 9AE. Tel. 071 629 4413.

Guildhall School of Music and Drama, Barbican, London EC2Y 8DT. Tel. 071 628 2571.

Musicians' Union, 60-62 Clapham Road, London SW9 0JJ. Tel. 071 582 5566.

Royal Scottish Academy of Music and Drama, School of Music, 100 Renfrew Street, Glasgow G2 3DB. Tel. 041 332 4101.

NATUROPATHY

General Council and Register of Naturopaths, 6 Netherhall Gardens, London NW3 5RR. Tel. 071 435 8728.

NURSERY NURSING

National Nursery Examination Board, 8 Chequer Street, St Albans, Hertfordshire AL1 3XZ. Tel. 0727 47636/7.

NURSING

England: **English National Board for Nursing, Midwifery and Health Visiting,** Careers Information Centre, PO Box 356, Sheffield S8 0SJ.

Wales: **Chief Nursing Officer,** Welsh Office, Cathays Park, Cardiff CF1 3NQ.

Scotland: **Nursing Adviser, Scottish Health Service Centre,** Crewe Road South, Edinburgh EH4 2LF.

Northern Ireland: **National Board for Nursing, Midwifery and Health Visiting,** RAC House, 79 Chichester Streeet, Belfast BT1 4JP.

NUTRITIONAL MEDICINE

College of Nutritional Medicine, East Bank, New Church Road, Smithills, Bolton BL1 5QP. Tel. 0204 492550.

OCCUPATIONAL THERAPY

College of Occupational Therapists, 20 Rede Place, London W2 4TU. Tel. 071 221 6599.

OPTICAL WORK

Association of British Dispensing Opticians, 6 Hurlingham Business Park, Sullivan Road, London SW6. Tel. 071 7636 0088/2.

British College of Optometrists, 10 Knaresborough Place, London SW5 0TG. Tel. 071 835 1302.

General Optical Council, 41 Harley Street, London W1N 2DJ. Tel. 071 580 3898.

OSTEOPATHY

British College of Naturopathy and Osteopathy, Frazer House, 6 Netherhall Gardens, London NW3 5RR. Tel. 071 435 8728.

European School of Osteopathy, 104 Tonbridge Road, Maidstone, Kent ME16 8SL. Tel. 0622 671558.

PHARMACY

Royal Pharmaceutical Society of Great Britain, 1 Lambeth High Street, London SE1 7JN. Tel. 071 735 9141, and 36 York Place, Edinburgh EH1 3HU. Tel. 031 556 4386.
National Pharmaceutical Association, Training Department, Mallinson House, 40-42 St Peter's Street, St Albans, Hertfordshire AL1 3NP. Tel. 0727 832161.

PHOTOGRAPHY

British Institute of Professional Photography, 2 Amwell End, Ware, Herts. SG12 9HN. Tel. 0920 464011.
Royal Photographic Society, The Octagon, Milsom Street, Bath BA1 1DN. Tel. 0225 462841.

PHYSIOTHERAPY

Chartered Society of Physiotherapy, 14 Bedford Row, London WC1R 4ED. Tel 071 242 1941.

PLAYGROUP ORGANISER

Pre-School Playgroup Association, 61-63 King's Cross Road, London WC1X 9LL. Tel. 071 833 0991.

POLICE

British Transport Police, PO Box 260, 15 Tavistock Place, London WC1H 9SJ. Tel. 071 388 7541.
Ministry of Defence Police, Recruitment Department, Medmenham, Marlow, Buckinghamshire SL7 2ED. Tel. 0628 471711.
Police Recruitment Department, Home Office, 50 Queen Anne's Gate, London SW1H 9AT. Tel. 071 273 3000.
Police Division, Scottish Home and Health Department, St Andrews House, Edinburgh EH1 3DE. Tel. 031 556 8400.

POLITICS

European Parliament, London Office, 2 Queen Anne's Gate, London SW1H 9AA. Tel. 071 222 0411.
House of Commons, Public Information Department, 1 Derby Gate, London SW1A 2DG. Tel. 071 219 5674.

POST OFFICE

Post Office Counters Ltd., Business Headquarters, Room 417, Drury House, 1-16 Blackfriars Road, London SE1 9UA. Tel. 071 922 1107.

POTTERY

Craft Potters Association, William Blake House, Marshall Street, London W1V 1FD. Tel. 071 437 7605.

PRISON SERVICE

HM Prison Service, Cleland House, Page Street, London SW1P 4LN. Tel. 071 217 3000.
Scottish Prison Service, Carlton House, 5 Redheughs Rigg, Edinburgh EH12 9HW. Tel. 031 244 8590.

PRIVATE INVESTIGATOR

Association of British Investigators, ABI House, 10 Bonner Hill Road, Kingston-upon-Thames, Surrey KT1 3EP. Tel. 081 546 3368.

PROBATION SERVICE

Probation Service Division, Home Office, Queen Anne's Gate, London SW1H 9AT. Tel. 071 273 3000.

PSYCHOLOGY

British Psychological Society, 48 Princess Road East, Leicester LE1 7DR. Tel. 0533 549568.

PSYCHOTHERAPY

British Association of Psychotherapists, 37 Mapesbury Road, London NW2 4HJ. Tel. 081 452 9823.

PUBLIC RELATIONS

Institute of Public Relations, The Old Trading House, 15 Northburgh Street, London EC1V 0PR. Tel. 071 253 5151.

PUBLISHING

Independent Publishers Guild, 25 Cambridge Road, Hampton, Middlesex TW12 2JL. Tel. 081 979 0250.

Publishers Assocation, 19 Bedford Square, London WC1B 3HJ. Tel. 071 580 6321/5.

PUBLIC HOUSES

Association of Valuers of Licensed Property, 18 Bloomsbury Square, London WC1A 2NS. Tel. 071 636 8992.

Brewers' Society Training Centre Ltd., 42 Portman Square, London W1H 0BB. Tel. 071 486 4831.

British Institute of Innkeeping, 51-53 High Street, Camberley, Surrey GU15 3RG. Tel. 0276 684449.

National Licensed Victuallers Association, Boardman House, 2 Downing Street, Farnham, Surrey GU9 7NX. Tel. 0252 714448.

Scottish Licensed Trade Association, 10 Walker Street, Edinburgh EH3 6QH. Tel. 031 225 5169.

RADIOGRAPHY

College of Radiographers, 14 Upper Wimpole Street, London W1M 8BN. Tel. 071 935 5726/7.

RAILWAYS

Recruitment: Manager, BR Board, Euston House, 24 Eversholt Street, London NW1 1DZ. Tel. 071 928 5151.

London Underground Recruitment: Selection Services Manager, Station Approach, Baker Street Station, Marylebone Road, London NW1 5LD. Tel. 071 222 5600.

REFLEXOLOGY

British School of Reflexology, Holistic Healing Centre, 92 Sheering Road, Old Harlow, Essex CM17 0JW. Tel. 0279 429060.

Dalamore School of Advanced Reflexology, 9 Mead Road, Shenley, Radlett, Hertfordshire WD7 9DA. Tel. 081 450 0454.

RELIGIOUS MINISTRY

Baptist Union of Great Britain, Ministry Office, Baptist House, 129 Broadway, PO Box 44, Didcot, Oxfordshire OX11 8RT. Tel. 0235 512077.

Church of England, Advisory Council for the Church's Ministry, Church House, Great Smith Street, London SW1P 3NZ. Tel. 071 222 9011.

Congregational Federation, The Congregational Centre, 4 Castle

Gate, Nottingham NG1 7AS. Tel. 0602 413801.

Methodist Church, Division of Ministries, 1 Central Buildings, London SW1H 9NH. Tel. 071 222 8010.

Roman Catholic Church, Fr. David Smith, Secretary, Vocations Directors, National Vocations Centre, 31 Moor Road, Leeds LS6 4BG. Tel. 0532 304434.

Salvation Army International Headquarters, 101 Queen Victoria Street, London EC4P 4EP. Tel. 071 236 5222.

Unitarian and Free Christian Churches, Essex Hall, 106 Essex Street, Strand, London WC2R 3HY. Tel. 071 240 2384/5.

United Reformed Church, Ministries Department, 86 Tavistock Place, London WC1H 9RT. Tel. 071 837 7661.

RETAILING

College for the Distributive Trades, 30 Leicester Square, London WC2H 7LE. Tel. 071 839 1547.

National Association of Shopkeepers, 91 Mansfield Road, Nottingham, NG1 3FN. Tel. 0602 475046.

SECURITY WORK

International Professional Security Association, 292A Torquay Road, Paignton, Devon TQ3 2ET. Tel. 0803 554849.

SHIATSU

British School of Shiatsu-Do, East West Centre, 188 Old Street, London EC1V 9BP. Tel. 071 251 0831.

Shiatsu Society, 14 Oakdene Road, Redhill, Surey RH1 6BT. Tel. 0737 767896.

SINGING

National Opera Studio, Morley College, 61 Westminster Bridge Road, London SE1 7HT. Tel. 071 261 9267.

SOCIAL AND COMMUNITY WORK

Central Council for Education and Training in Social Work (CCETSW), Derbyshire House, St Chad's Street, London WC1H 8AD. Tel. 071 278 2455; Ivanhoe House, 9 South St David Street, Edinbugh EH2 2BW. Tel. 031 556 2953; West Wing, St. David's House, Wood Street, Cardiff CF1 1ES. Tel. 0222 26257; 14 Malone Road, Belfast BT9 5BN. Tel. 0232 665 390.

Council for Education and Training in Youth and Community Work, Wellington House, Wellington Street, Leicester LE1 6HL. Tel. 0533 558763.

SPEECH THERAPY

College of Speech Therapists, Harold Poster House, 6 Lechmere Road, London NW2 5BU. Tel. 081 459 8521.

SPORTS COACHING

National Coaching Foundation, 4 College Close, Beckett Park, Leeds LS6 3QH. Tel. 0532 744802.

Sports Council, 16 Upper Woburn Place, London WC1H 0QP. Tel. 071 388 1277.

Scottish Sports Council, Caledonia House, South Gyle, Edinburgh EH12 9DQ. Tel. 031 317 7200.

SURVEYING

Royal Institute of Chartered Surveyors, 12 Great George Street, London SW1 3AD. Tel. 071 222 7000.

Society for Surveying Technicians, Drayton House, 30 Gordon Street, London WC1H 0AX. Tel. 071 338 8008.

TAXI DRIVER

Licenced Taxi Drivers' Assocation, 9-11 Woodfield Road, London W9 2BA. Tel. 071 286 1046.

TEACHING

TASC Publicity Unit, Department of Education, Sanctuary Buildings, Great Smith Street, London SW1 3BT. Tel. 071 925 5000.

Scottish Education Department, New St Andrew's House, St James' Centre, Edinburgh EH1 3SY. Tel. 031 557 0050.

Northern Ireland Education Department, Rathgael House, Balloo Road, Bangor, Co. Down BT19 2PR. Tel. 0247 270077.

TELEVISION

(see *Films and TV*).

THATCHER

Thatching Advisory Services Ltd., Rose Tree Farm, 29 Nine Mile Ride, Finchampstead, Wokingham, Berkshire RG11 4QD. Tel. 0734 734203.

TOASTMASTER

Guild of Professional Toastmasters, 12 Little Bornes, Alleyn Park, London SE21 8SE. Tel. 081 670 5585.

TRADING STANDARDS OFFICER

Institute of Trading Standards Administration, 4/5 Hadleigh Business Centre, 351 London Road, Hadleigh, Essex SS7 2BT. Tel. 0702 559922.

TRANSLATOR/INTERPRETER

Association Internationale des Interpretes de Conferences (AIIC), 14 rue de l'Ancien Port, CH 1201, Geneve, Switzerland. Tel. 010 41 22 7313323.
Institute of Linguists, 24A Highbury Grove, London N5 2EA. Tel. 071 359 7445.

TRAVEL AND TOURISM

Association of British Travel Agents (ABTA), 55-57 Newman Street, London W1P 4AH. Tel 071 637 2444; **National Training Board,** 11-17 Chertsey Road, Woking, Surrey GU21 5AL. Tel. 0486 22732.
Civil Aviation Authority, ATOL Section, CAA House, 45-59 Kingsway, London WC2B 6TE. Tel. 071 832 5620.
International Air Transport Association (IATA), 15 Kingsway London WC2B 6UN. Tel. 071 497 1048.
Guild of Guide Lecturers, 2 Bridge Street, London SW1A 2JR. Tel. 071 839 7438.

TRICHOLOGY

Institute of Trichologists, 228 Stockwell Road, London SW9 9SU. Tel. 071 733 2056.

WINE PRODUCTION

English Vineyards Association Limited, 38 West Park, London

SE9 4RH. Tel. 081 857 0452.

YOUTH WORK

(see *Social and community work*).

Further Reading

Most of the books and journals listed in this selective bibliography should be available in public libraries. Check in particular the directories which appear under the Careers heading.

A wide range of books devoted to specific careers are available in series produced by such publishers as Kogan Page (*'Careers in...'*) Cassell (*'Getting a Job in...'*) and Batsford (*'Working in...'*). Your local library will almost certainly stock a selection of these.

Helpful materials on a variety of different careers are published by the Careers and Occupational Information Centre (COIC) and the Association of Graduate Careers Advisory Services (AGCA), who will be glad to send you lists of their titles (see under Careers in the Useful Addresses list).

Abroad, working:
Daily Telegraph guide to working abroad, G Goltzen (Kogan Page).
The Expatriate (monthly).
Getting a Job in Europe, P. Riley (Northcote).

Accountancy
Accountancy Age (weekly).
Accounting (weekly).

Acting:
The Actors Handbook, B Turner (Bloomsbury).
(see also *Performing arts*)

Advertising:
Ogilvy on Advertising, D Ogilvy (Pan).
Campaign (weekly).

Animals:
Dog World (weekly).

Kennel Gazette (monthly).
Cat World (monthly).

Antiques:
Miller's Antiques Price Guide (Millers Publications).
Antiques Trade Gazette (weekly).

Archaeology:
Archaeology: an introduction, K Greene (Batsford).

Architecture:
Architects' Journal (weekly).
Architectural Review (monthly).

Bookshops:
The Bookseller (weekly).

Building industry:
Building (weekly).

Business:
Going for it: How to Succeed as an Entrepreneur, V Kiam (Collins).
Be Your Own Boss: starter kit (National Extension College).
101 Great Money-Making Ideas, M. Hempshell (Northcote).
Running Your Own Business, R Edwards (Oyez Longman).
Starting a Business on a Shoestring, M. Syrett & C Dunn (Northcote/Penguin).
The Small Business Handbook, B Wilson, ed. (Blackwell).

Careers, general:
Careers '92 (COIC).
Careers Encyclopaedia (Cassells).
Job File '92 (Hodder and Stoughton).
The Alternative Careers Book, K Boehm and J Lees-Spalding (Papermac).
Equal Opportunities, A Alston (Penguin).
British Qualifications (Kogan Page).
(see also *Job finding*).

Clothes shop:
  Clothing Industry Yearbook (British Clothing Industry Association).
  Fashion Weekly.
  Draper's Record (weekly).

Complementary medicine:
  Alternative Medicine: a guide to natural therapies, A Stanway (Penguin).
  Start a Career in Alternative Medicine: a manual and directory of courses, G Maher (Tackmarsh).

Computing:
  Computer Weekly.
  Computing (weekly).

Confectioner, tobacconist, newsagent:
  CTN (weekly).

Conservation:
  Directory of Training Opportunities in Countryside Conservation & Recreation (Countryside Commission).

Construction industry:
  Construction Industry Handbook of Professional and Management Careers, Construction Industry Training Board (Hobsons).

Counselling:
  On Being a Counsellor, E Kennedy (Macmillan).
  Counselling and Psychotherapy Resources Directory (British Association for Counselling).

Crafts:
  The Complete Practical Book of Country Crafts, J Hill (David and Charles).
  Crafts (bi-monthly).

Dancing:
  Dancing Times (monthly).

Design:
  Design Week.
  Design (monthly).

Education:
  UCCA/PCAS guides.
  Colleges and Institutes of Higher Education Guide (Standing Conference of Principals, Edge Hill College of Education, Ormskirk, Lancashire. L39 4QP).
  Access to Higher Education (ECCTIS).
  Second Chances: guide to adult education and training, A Pates and M Good (COIC).
  Mature Students Handbook, M Korving (Kogan Page).
  The Potter Guide to Higher Education, S Potter & P Clare (Dalebank Books).
  Handbook of Degree and Advanced Courses (NATFHE).
  University Entrance: the Official Guide, CVCP (Sheed and Ward).
  Directory of Grantmaking Trusts (Charities Aid Foundation, annual).
  Charities Digest (Family Welfare Association).
  Free publications:
  Mature Students: Universities Welcome You, CVCP, 29 Tavistock Square, London WC1H 9EZ.
  The Mature Applicant's Guide to Scottish Degree Courses, Careers Information Unit, Education Department, Fife Regional Council, Albany House, Glenrothes, Fife KY7 5NZ.
  Grants to Students: a brief guide, DES, Publications Despatch Centre, Honeypot Lane, Canons Park, Stanmore, Middlesex HA7 1AZ; Northern Ireland: Department of Education Scholarships Branch, Rathgael House, Balloo House, Bangor, County Down BT19 2PR.
  Loans for Students: a brief guide, DES, Publications Despatch Centre (address as previous entry).
  Guide to Students' Allowances, Scottish Education Department Awards Branch, Gyleview House, 3 Redheughs Rigg, South Gyle, Edinburgh EH12 9HH.
  Which Benefit? a pocket guide to social security (Local DSS offices).

Employment agencies:
Yearbook of Recruitment and Employment Agencies, AP Information Services Ltd. (Longman).

Engineering:
The Engineer (weekly).

Estate agency:
Estates Gazette (weekly).

Farming:
Farming UK (HMSO).
Farmers Weekly.
Farming News (weekly).
Smallholder (monthly).

Farriery:
Forge 88 (bi-monthly).

Films and television:
Screen International (weekly).

Financial adviser:
Financial Times (daily).
Investors Chronicle (weekly).

Franchises:
Franchise Handbook (CGB Publishing).
UK Franchise Directory (Franchise Development Services).

Genealogy:
Family Tree Magazine (monthly).

Graphology:
The Secret Self: a comprehensive guide to handwriting analysis, A Koren (Adama Books).

Hairdressing:
Hairdressers Journal International (weekly).

Home economics:
Careers and Courses in Home Economics, J Lane (Hobson).

Homeopathy:
The Science of Homeopathy, G Vithoukas (Dawson Publications).

Horticulture:
Horticulture Week.

Hotels and catering:
Catering and Hotelkeeping as a Career (Barrie and Jenkins).
Caterer and Hotelkeeeper (weekly).

Hypnotherapy:
Hypnosis, U Markham (Macdonald Optima).

Insurance:
Insurance Age (monthly).
Insurance Brokers Monthly.

Jewellery:
Retail Jeweller (fortnightly).

Job finding:
Changing Your Job after 35: Daily Telegraph Guide, G Golzen and P Plumbley (Kogan Page).
Returning to Work, Women Returners Network (Longmans).
Preparing Your Own CV, R Corfield (Kogan Page).
(see also *Careers).*

Journalism:
Willings' Press Guide.
UK Press Gazette (weekly).

Law:
Solicitors' Journal (weekly).

Local government:
Municipal Yearbook.
Local Government Chronicle (weekly).
Local Government Review (weekly).

Management and administration:
Administrator (monthly).

Marketing:
Marketing Week.

Medicine:
Learning Medicine, P Richards (BMA).

Middle age:
Making the Most of Middle Age, Dr B Pitt (Sheldon Press).
The Prime of Your Life, Dr M Stoppard (Penguin).
Half Way, Bishop Jim Thompson (Collins Fount).
How to Survive Middle Age, C Matthew (Pavilion).
Forty Plus, M Batchelor (Lion).
Men at Mid-life, J Clay (Sidgwick and Jackson).

Museums:
Palaces of Discovery: the changing world of Britain's Museums,
S Tait (Quiller Press).
Museum Yearbook (Rhinegold Publishing Ltd).

Music:
Musicians Handbook (Rhinegold Publishing Ltd).
Music and Musicians (monthly).

Nursing:
Nursing Times (weekly).
Nursing Standard (weekly).

Optical work:
The Optician (weekly).

Osteopath
Osteopathy, S Sandler (Pan).

Performing arts:
British Performing Arts Yearbook (Rhinegold Publishing Ltd).
Stage and Television Today (weekly).
(See also *Acting*).

Pharmacy:
  Pharmaceutical Journal (weekly).

Photography:
  Freelance Photographer's Market Handbook, J Tracey and S Gibson, eds (Bureau of Freelance Photographers).
  The Photographer (monthly).

Police:
  Police and Constabulary Almanac (R Hazell and Co.).

Politics:
  Statesmen's Yearbook.
  House Magazine (weekly when the House of Commons is sitting).

Private investigator:
  The Investigator, J Ackroyd (Muller).

Psychotherapy:
  The Art of Psychotherapy, A Storr (Penguin).

Public houses:
  Morning Advertiser (daily).
  Licensee (monthly).

Public relations:
  PR Week.

Publishing:
  The Truth About Publishing, S Unwin (Penguin).
  Directory of Publishing (Cassells and Publishers Association).
  Publishing News (weekly).
  The Bookseller (weekly).

Railways:
  Railway Gazette International (monthly).

Reflexology:
  Reflexology, T Unwin and J M Foulkes (Cockatrice Press).

Religious ministry:
UK Christian Handbook, P Brierley and D Longley, eds (MARC European/Evangelical Alliance/Bible Society).

Social work:
Social Work Today (weekly).

Teaching:
NATFHE handbook of initial teacher training.
Times Educational Supplement (weekly).

Thatcher:
Thatch, B West (David and Charles).

Travel:
Handbook of Tourism and Leisure, English Tourist Board (Hobsons).
Travel Trade Gazette (weekly).
Travel News (weekly).

Visual arts:
The Artists' Directory, H Waddell and R Layzell (A and C Black).
The Artist (monthly).

Wine production:
Vine Growing in Britain, G Pearkes (J M Dent).
The New English Vineyard, J Smith (Sidgwick and Jackson).
Wine (monthly).

Writing:
The Writers and Artists Year Book (A and C Black).
The Writer's Handbook (Macmillan).

Yoga:
Light on Yoga, B K S Iyengar (Allen and Unwin).

Index

Abroad, working 145-52
Accountancy 29-30
Acting 140-1
Acupuncture 74-5
Administration 27-33
Advertising 57-8
Alternative medicine 73-80
Agriculture 97-102
Ambulance Service 65
Anglican Communion 84
Animals, careers with 106-10
  breeding/showing 109
  training 109-10
  welfare work 107
Antiques 36
  dealer 36
  restoration 134
Archaeology 63-4
Architecture 49
Archivist 62-3
Armed forces 96
Aromatherapy 75
Arts administration 111
Audiology 65-6
Australia 150-1

Bakery 36-7
Baptists 88-9
Barrister 91
Basketry 134
Beauty and grooming 121-2
Boat services 113-4
Bookshop 37-8
British Council 147
Building trades 51
Bus driver 46
Butcher 38

Butler 126

Canada 150-1
Careers adviser 124-5
Catering business 118
Ceramics 134
Charities 83-4
Chauffeur/chauffeuse 124
Childminding 126-7
Chiropody 66
Chiropractic 75
Church of England 85-6
Civil Service 33
Clerical work 28
Clothes shop 38-9
Coach driver 46
Coastguard 95
Commonwealth recruitment 147
Community work 81
Company secretary 27
Complementary medicine 73-80
Computers 28
Confectioner, tobacconist, newsagent 39-40
Congregationalists 89
Conservation 106, 132
Construction industry 51
Correspondence colleges 56
Courier services 48
Counselling 82-3
Crafts 133-5
Creative writing 136-40
  comedy 139
  novels 136-8
  plays 139
  poetry 138

sources of help 139
CTN, *see Confectioner, tobacconist, newsagent*
Customs & Excise officer 95

Dancing 144
Degree course 16-26
Dentistry 66-7
Design 132-3
Dietetics 67
Diplomatic Service 148
Distribution, *see Transport and distribution*
DIY/hardware shop 40
Dog warden 108
Driving 122-4
  examiner 123-4
  instructor 122-3

Education, returning to 16-26
Emigration 149-52
Employment agency 124-5
Engineering 51-2
Environmental health officer 95
Escort agency 126
Estate agency 50
European Community 148-9
Export 45

Farming 97-102
Farriery 107
Fashion design 132-3
Films and television 59
Financial adviser 32-3
Floristry 41
Forestry 105
Fostering 83
Franchises 44
Funeral work 127

Garden centres 103
Gardening 104

Genealogy 127-8
Government agencies, *see Working abroad*
Graphology 128
Guide dog training 106-7

Hairdressing 121-2
Hardware shop, *see DIY*
Health 65-80
  NHS management professions 65-80
Heavy goods driver 46
Helping hand services 128
Herbalism 75-6
Homeopathy 67
Home economics 118-9
Horticulture 102-4
Hospitality industry 115-9
Hotels 117
Hypnotherapy 76-7

Immigration officer 95
Insurance 30-31
  broker 31-32
  salesperson 30-1
Interior design 132-3
Interpreter, see *Translator*
Introduction agency 125-6

Jeweller 41
Job finding 13-14
Journalism 56-7

Languages, careers with 61-2
Law 91-6
Legal executive 92
Leisure industry 111
Librarian 62
Licensed conveyancer 93
Local government 33

Management 27-33

and administration 27-33
consultancy 28-9
Market research 45-6
Marketing consultant 44
Marriage bureau 125-6
Massage 77
Media and communications 56-61
Medical secretary 68
Medicine 62-8
Methodists 88
Military service 96
Museum 63
Music 142-4

New Zealand 150-1
Newsagent, see *Confectionery, tobacconist, newsagent*
Nurseries 54-5
Nursing 69-70
Nutritional medicine 78

Occupational therapy 70
Office work 27-33
Off-licence 41-2
Optical work 70-1
Osteopathy 78

Parkkeeper 94
Performing arts 140-4
Personal services 121-8
Pharmacy 71
Photography 60
Physiotherapy 71-2
Playgroup organiser 55
Poetry 138
Police 93
Politics 60-1
Post Office 47
Pottery 133
Prison service 96
Private investigator 94

Probation Service 82
Protection services 93-6
Psychology 72
Psychotherapy 72-3
Public relations 57
Publishing 58-9
Public houses 115-6

Radiography 73
Railways 47
Reflexology 78-9
Religious ministry 84-90
Religious orders 87
Restaurants 117-8
Retailing 35
Riding instructor 107
Road transport 46
Roman Catholic Church 86

Sales agent 43-4
Salvation Army 89-90
Sea-going careers 47
Secretarial work 28
Security work 93-4
Shiatsu 79-80
Singing 142
Solicitor 91-2
Social work 81-2
Sports coaching 114
Sub-post office 42-3
Surveying 49-50

Taxi driver 124
Teaching 53-6
    correspondence colleges 56
    further and higher education 55-6
    nursery nurse/playgroup organiser 55
    secondary and primary 53-4
TEFL 61-2
Television, see *Films*

Territorial Army 96
Thatching 135
Toastmaster 119
Tobacconist, *see Confectioner, tobacconist, newsagent*
Tour guide 111-3
Traffic warden 93
Trading standards officer 94
Translator 61
Transport and distribution 46-7
Travel and tourism 111-3
Trichology 121-2

Unitarian Church 89
United Nations 147
United Reform Church 88

Veterinary nurse 108
Video production 59
Visual arts 129-31
Voluntary work 84
   abroad 149

Wine production 104-5
Work study 28
Working abroad 145

Yoga 80
Youth and community work 82